Administration
in Early Education

Liz Jenkins

THOMSON

™

DELMAR LEARNING

Australia • Canada • Mexico • Singapore • Spain • United Kingdom • United States

THOMSON

DELMAR LEARNING

Printed in Canada

1 2 3 4 5 XXX 09 08 07 06

For more information contact Thomson Delmar Learning, Executive Woods, 5 Maxwell Drive, Clifton Park, NY 12065-2919.

Or find us on the World Wide Web at http://www.thomsonlearning.com, http://www.delmarlearning.com, or http://www.earlychilded.delmar.com

ISBN 1-4180-0174-0

Library of Congress Catalog Card Number: 2006001542

NOTICE TO THE READER

The authors and Thomson Delmar Learning affirm that the Web site URLs referenced herein were accurate at the time of printing. However, due to the fluid nature of the Internet, we cannot guarantee their accuracy for the life of the edition.

Join us on the Web at
EarlyChildEd.delmar.com

TABLE OF CONTENTS

This tool was developed to help you, the budding teacher and/or child care provider, as you move into your first classroom. The editors at Thomson Delmar Learning encourage and appreciate your feedback on this or any of our other products. Go to http://www.earlychilded.delmar.com and click on the Contact Us link.

INTRODUCTION

Throughout a college preparation program to become an early childhood educator, students take many courses and read many textbooks. Their knowledge grows as they accumulate ideas from lectures, reading, experiences, and discussions. When they finish their coursework, graduate, and move into their first teaching positions, students often leave behind some of the books they have used. The hope is, however, that they take with them the important ideas from their classes and books as they begin their own professional practice.

More experienced colleagues or mentors sometimes support teachers in their first teaching positions, helping them make the transition from the college classroom to being responsible for a group of young children. At other times, new teachers are left to travel their own paths, relying on their own resources. Whatever your situation, this professional enhancement guide is designed to provide reminders of what you have learned, as well as resources to help you make sense of and apply that knowledge.

Teachers of young children are under great pressure today. Families demand support in the difficult task of child-rearing in today's fast-paced and changing world. Some families become so overwhelmed with the tasks of parenting that they seem to leave too much responsibility on the shoulders of teachers and caregivers. From administrators and institutions, there are expectations that sometimes seem overwhelming. Teachers are being held accountable for children's learning in ways unprecedented in even the recent past. Public scrutiny has led to insistence on teaching practices that may seem contrary to the best interests of children or their teachers. New teachers may find themselves caught between the realities of the schools or centers where they are working, and their own philosophies and ideals of working with children. When faced with such dilemmas, these teachers need to be able to step back and reflect on what they know of best practices, renewing their professional determination to make appropriate decisions for children.

This book provides a tool for that reflection:

- Tips for getting off to a great start in your new environment

- Information about typical developmental patterns of children from birth through school age

- Suggestions for materials that promote development for children from infancy through the primary grades

- Tools to assist teachers in observing children and gathering data to help set appropriate goals for individual children

- Guides for planning appropriate classroom experiences and sample lesson plans

- Tips for introducing children to the joys of literacy

- A summary of the key ideas about developmentally appropriate practice, the process of decision making that allows teachers to provide optimum environments for children from birth through school age

- Professional development resources for teachers

- Ideas for locating lists of other resources

- Case studies of relevant, realistic situations you may face, as well as best practices for successfully navigating them

- Insight into issues and trends facing early childhood educators today

Becoming a teacher is a continuing process of growing, learning, reflecting, and discovering through experience. Having these resources will help you along your way. Good luck on your journey!

REFLECTIONS FOR GROWING TEACHERS

Administrators can make a real difference for teachers in early childhood programs by encouraging them to engage in reflective practice, thinking back over the events of a day, week, month, semester, or school year to build on past experience. Administrators can also benefit from reflecting on what has gone well and where improvement is possible as they seek to "grow" children and teachers and strengthen families.

Teachers spend most of their time working directly with young children and their families. During the day, questions and concerns arise and decisions have to be made, meaning teachers must always be reflective about their work. Too often, teachers believe they are too busy to spend time thinking, but experienced professional teachers have learned that reflection sustains their best work. Growing teachers need regular time to consider the questions and concerns that arise from their practice. Some teachers use journals to keep track of the process. An effective administrator could provide teachers with an attractive, inviting journal as a part of the orientation kit each teacher receives at hire or at the start of a new school year.

These questions can be used to begin your reflection. Add questions from your own experience. Remember, these are not questions to be answered once and forgotten; review these questions often.

QUESTIONS FOR DAILY REFLECTION

This day would have been better if_____

_____.

One quote that I like to keep in mind is _____

_____.

One way I can help my children feel more competent is _____

_____.

QUESTIONS FOR WEEKLY REFLECTION

One new thing I think I'll try this week is _____

_____.

The highlight of this week was _____

_____.

The observations this week made me think more about _____

_____.

I loved my job this week when _____

_____.

I hated my job this week when _____

_____.

One thing I can try to make better next week is _____

_____.

The funniest thing I heard a child say this week was_____

_____.

QUESTIONS FOR MONTHLY REFLECTION

I think I need to know more about_____

_____.

I just don't understand why _____

_____.

The family member I feel most comfortable with is _____

_____.

And I think the reason for that is _____

_____.

The family member I feel least comfortable with is _____

_____.

And I think the reason for that is _____

_____.

What have I done lately to spark the children's imagination and creativity?_____

_____.

QUESTIONS FOR YEARLY REFLECTION

I think my favorite creative activity this year was _____

_____.

Has my attitude about teaching changed this year? Why?_____

_____.

When next year starts, one thing I will do more of is _____

_____.

When next year starts, one thing I won't do is _____

_____.

QUESTIONS FOR REFLECTION AFTER THE FIRST SEMESTER OF TEACHING

One area where my teaching is changing is _____

_____.

One area where my teaching needs to change is _____

_____.

The biggest gains in learning have been made by _____

_____.

And I think that this is because _____

_____.

I'm working on a bad habit of_____

_____.

Dealing with_____ is the most difficult thing I had to face recently
because   _____

_____.

My teaching style has been most influenced by _____

_____.

I really need to start_____

_____.

When children have difficulty sharing, I _____

_____.

Something I enjoy that I could share with my class is _____

_____.

QUESTIONS FOR REFLECTION AFTER TWO OR MORE YEARS OF EXPERIENCE

If I were going to advise a new teacher, the most helpful piece of advice would be

_____

_____.

I've been trying to facilitate friendships among the children by _____

_____.

In thinking more about math and science in my curriculum, I believe_____

_____.

I used to _____ but now I_____

_____.

The child who has helped me learn the most is _____.
I learned _____

_____.

I've grown in my communication by _____

_____.

The best thing I've learned by observing is _____.

_____.

I still don't understand why _____

_____.

One mistake I used to make that I don't make any longer is _____

_____.

QUESTIONS YOU WANT TO ASK YOURSELF

_____

_____

_____

_____

_____

_____

Adapted from Nilsen, B. A., *Week by Week: Documenting the Development of Young Children,*
3E, published by Thomson Delmar Learning.

TIPS FOR SUCCESS

As an administrator, you can help new teachers get off to a good start by sharing these tips for success with them. Remember that the best way to convey each of these ideas to faculty is to be an excellent role model of the concept yourself. Your employees will learn more from what you do than from what you say. Remember, too, that you are a role model for the children. They are constantly watching how you dress, what you say, and what you do.

BE A PROFESSIONAL

- Dress conservatively and follow your employer's clothing expectations (which could include wearing closed-toe shoes to be safe and active with children and wearing clean, modest, and comfortable clothing).

- Be prepared and on time.

- Avoid excessive absences.

- Use appropriate language with children and adults.

- Be positive when talking to parents and show that you are forming a positive relationship with their children; "catch children doing something right" and share those accomplishments. Challenges with children can be discussed after you have established trust with the parents.

BE A TEAM PLAYER

- Rely on team members to help you learn the parameters of your new position.

- Don't be afraid to ask questions or request guidance from teammates.

- Show your support and be responsible.

- Step in to do your share of the work; don't expect others to clean up after you.

- Help others whenever possible.

- Respect others' ideas and avoid telling them how to do things.

- Strive to balance your ability to make decisions with following the lead of others.

LEARN ABOUT CHILDREN

- Be aware of children's physical, social, emotional, and cognitive development.

- Assess children's development and plan curriculum that will enhance it.

- Be aware that children will test you! (Children, especially school age, will expect that you don't know the rules and may try to convince you to let them do things that were not previously allowed.)

- Never hesitate to double-check something with teammates when in doubt.

- Use positive management techniques with children.

MANAGEMENT TECHNIQUES FOR GAINING CHILDREN'S COOPERATION

Many techniques are available to help children cooperate. Children need respectful reminders of expectations and adult support to help them meet those expectations. Be sure that your expectations are age appropriate and individually appropriate. These techniques are more preventive in nature:

- Use positive phrases and state exactly what you expect children to do. "Stand by the door" is more effective than "Don't go outside until everyone is ready."

- Avoid "no" and "don't." Be clear about what you want children to do, not what you don't want them to do.

- Sequence directions using the "When-then" phrase; for example, "When things are put away where they belong, then we can go outside."

- Stay close. Merely standing near children can be enough to help them manage behavior. Be aware, however, that if you are talking to another adult, children may act out because they know they do not have your attention.

- Offer sufficient and appropriate choices. Children need a variety of activities that interest them and that will create opportunities for success.

GETTING STARTED

There is always an array of information to learn when starting in a new position working with children. Use this fill-in-the blank section to customize this resource book to your specific environment.

What are the school's or center's hours of operation?

On school days: _____

_____

_____

On vacation days: _____

_____

_____

What is the basic daily schedule and what are my responsibilities during each time segment?

_____

_____

_____

_____

_____

_____

What are the procedures for checking children in and out of the program?

_____

_____

Do I call if I have to be absent? Who is my contact?

Name:_____

Phone number: _____

What is the dress code for employees?

_____

_____

For what basic health and safety practices will I be responsible? Where are the materials stored for this? (Bleach, gloves, etc.)

Sanitizing tables: _____

_____

_____

_____

Cleaning and maintaining equipment and materials: _____

_____

_____

_____

What are the emergency procedures?

Mildly injured child: _____

_____

_____

_____

_____

Earthquake/tornado: _____

_____

_____

_____

_____

_____

_____

Fire: _____

_____

_____

_____

_____

_____

First aid: _____

_____

_____

_____

_____

Other: _____

_____

_____

_____

_____

DEVELOPMENTAL MILESTONES BY AGE

Whether you are working with infants, toddlers, preschoolers, or primary-aged children, your first requirement is to know how children develop and learn. In your college program, you no doubt studied child development. The following is a shortened version of the universal steps most children go through as they develop. Some children move easily from one step to another, whereas other children move forward in one area but lag behind in others. Use these milestones as a guide for arranging an environment or planning activities in your room.

Child's Name _____   Age _____
Observer _____   Date _____

Developmental Checklist (by six months)

Does the child . . .	Yes	No	Sometimes
1. Show continued gains in height, weight, and head circumference?	☐	☐	☐
2. Reach for toys or objects when they are presented?	☐	☐	☐
3. Begin to roll from stomach to back?	☐	☐	☐
4. Sit with minimal support?	☐	☐	☐
5. Transfer objects from one hand to the other?	☐	☐	☐
6. Raise up on arms, lifting head and chest, when placed on stomach?	☐	☐	☐
7. Babble, coo, and imitate sounds?	☐	☐	☐
8. Turn to locate the source of a sound?	☐	☐	☐
9. Focus on an object and follow its movement vertically and horizontally?	☐	☐	☐
10. Exhibit a blink reflex?	☐	☐	☐
11. Enjoy being held and cuddled?	☐	☐	☐

Developmental Checklist, continued			
Does the child . . .	Yes	No	Sometimes
12. Recognize and respond to familiar faces?	☐	☐	☐
13. Begin sleeping six to eight hours through the night?	☐	☐	☐
14. Suck vigorously when it is time to eat?	☐	☐	☐
15. Enjoy playing in water during bath time?	☐	☐	☐

DEVELOPMENTAL ALERTS

Check with a health care provider or early childhood specialist if, by *one month* of age, the infant *does not*

- show alarm or "startle" responses to loud noise.
- suck and swallow with ease.
- show gains in height, weight, and head circumference.
- grasp with equal strength with both hands.
- make eye-to-eye contact when awake and being held.
- become quiet soon after being picked up.
- roll head from side to side when placed on stomach.
- express needs and emotions with cries and patterns of vocalizations that can be distinguished from one another.
- stop crying when picked up and held.

DEVELOPMENTAL ALERTS

Check with a health care provider or early childhood specialist if, by *four months* of age, the infant *does not*

- continue to show steady increases in height, weight, and head circumference.
- smile in response to the smiles of others (the social smile is a significant developmental milestone).
- follow a moving object with eyes focusing together.

- bring hands together mid-chest.

- turn head to locate sounds.

- begin to raise head and upper body when placed on stomach.

- reach for objects or familiar persons.

Child's Name _____   Age _____

Observer _____   Date _____

Developmental Checklist (by 12 months)

Does the child . . .	Yes	No	Sometimes
1. Walk with assistance?	☐	☐	☐
2. Roll a ball in imitation of an adult?	☐	☐	☐
3. Pick objects up with thumb and forefinger?	☐	☐	☐
4. Transfer objects from one hand to the other?	☐	☐	☐
5. Pick up dropped toys?	☐	☐	☐
6. Look directly at adult's face?	☐	☐	☐
7. Imitate gestures: peek-a-boo, bye-bye, pat-a-cake?	☐	☐	☐
8. Find object hidden under a cup?	☐	☐	☐
9. Feed self crackers (munching, not sucking on them)?	☐	☐	☐
10. Hold cup with two hands; drink with assistance?	☐	☐	☐
11. Smile spontaneously?	☐	☐	☐
12. Pay attention to own name?	☐	☐	☐
13. Respond to "no"?	☐	☐	☐
14. Respond differently to strangers and familiar persons?	☐	☐	☐
15. Respond differently to sounds: vacuum, phone, door?	☐	☐	☐
16. Look at person who speaks to him or her?	☐	☐	☐
17. Respond to simple directions accompanied by gestures?	☐	☐	☐
18. Make several consonant–vowel combination sounds?	☐	☐	☐
19. Vocalize back to person who has talked to him or her?	☐	☐	☐
20. Use intonation patterns that sound like scolding, asking, exclaiming?	☐	☐	☐
21. Say "da-da" or "ma-ma"?	☐	☐	☐

DEVELOPMENTAL ALERTS

Check with a health care provider or early childhood specialist if, by 12 *months* of age, the infant *does not*

- blink when fast-moving objects approach the eyes.

- begin to cut teeth.

- imitate simple sounds.

- follow simple verbal requests: "come," "bye-bye."

- pull self to a standing position.

Child's Name _____   Age _____

Observer _____   Date _____

Developmental Checklist (by two years)

Does the child . . .	Yes	No	Sometimes
1. Walk alone?	☐	☐	☐
2. Bend over and pick up toy without falling over?	☐	☐	☐
3. Seat self in child-size chair? Walk up and down stairs with assistance?	☐	☐	☐
4. Place several rings on a stick?	☐	☐	☐
5. Place five pegs in a pegboard?	☐	☐	☐
6. Turn pages two or three at a time?	☐	☐	☐
7. Scribble?	☐	☐	☐
8. Follow one-step direction involving something familiar: "Give me _____." "Show me _____." "Get a _____."?	☐	☐	☐
9. Match familiar objects?	☐	☐	☐
10. Use spoon with some spilling?	☐	☐	☐
11. Drink from cup holding it with one hand, unassisted?	☐	☐	☐
12. Chew food?	☐	☐	☐
13. Take off coat, shoe, sock?	☐	☐	☐
14. Zip and unzip large zipper?	☐	☐	☐
15. Recognize self in mirror or picture?	☐	☐	☐
16. Refer to self by name?	☐	☐	☐
17. Imitate adult behaviors in play—for example, feeds "baby"?	☐	☐	☐
18. Help put things away?	☐	☐	☐

Developmental Checklist, continued

Does the child . . .	Yes	No	Sometimes
19. Respond to specific words by showing what was named: toy, pet, family member?	☐	☐	☐
20. Ask for desired items by name: (for example, cookie)?	☐	☐	☐
21. Answer with name of object when asked "What's that"?	☐	☐	☐
22. Make some two-word statements: "Daddy bye-bye"?	☐	☐	☐

DEVELOPMENTAL ALERTS

Check with a health care provider or early childhood specialist if, by *twenty four months* of age, the child *does not*

- attempt to talk or repeat words.

- understand some new words.

- respond to simple questions with "yes" or "no."

- walk alone (or with very little help).

- exhibit a variety of emotions: anger, delight, fear.

- show interest in pictures.

- recognize self in mirror.

- attempt self-feeding: hold own cup to mouth and drink.

Child's Name _____   Age _____
Observer _____   Date _____

Developmental Checklist (by three years)

Does the child . . .	Yes	No	Sometimes
1. Run well in a forward direction?	☐	☐	☐
2. Jump in place, two feet together?	☐	☐	☐
3. Walk on tiptoe?	☐	☐	☐
4. Throw ball (but without direction or aim)?	☐	☐	☐
5. Kick ball forward?	☐	☐	☐
6. String four large beads?	☐	☐	☐
7. Turn pages in book singly?	☐	☐	☐
8. Hold crayon: imitate circular, vertical, horizontal strokes?	☐	☐	☐

Developmental Checklist, continued

Does the child . . .	Yes	No	Sometimes
9. Match shapes?	☐	☐	☐
10. Demonstrate number concepts of 1 and 2?; (Can select 1 or 2; can tell if one or two objects.)	☐	☐	☐
11. Use spoon without spilling?	☐	☐	☐
12. Drink from a straw?	☐	☐	☐
13. Put on and take off coat?	☐	☐	☐
14. Wash and dry hands with some assistance?	☐	☐	☐
15. Watch other children; play near them; sometimes join in their play?	☐	☐	☐
16. Defend own possessions?	☐	☐	☐
17. Use symbols in play—for example, tin pan on head becomes helmet and crate becomes a spaceship?	☐	☐	☐
18. Respond to "Put _____ in the box," "Take the _____ out of the box"?	☐	☐	☐
19. Select correct item on request: big versus little; one versus two?	☐	☐	☐
20. Identify objects by their use: show own shoe when asked, "What do you wear on your feet?"	☐	☐	☐
21. Ask questions?	☐	☐	☐
22. Tell about something with functional phrases that carry meaning: "Daddy go airplane"; "Me hungry now"?	☐	☐	☐

DEVELOPMENTAL ALERTS

Check with a health care provider or early childhood specialist if, by the *third* birthday, the child *does not*

- eat a fairly well-rounded diet, even though amounts are limited.

- walk confidently with few stumbles or falls; climb steps with help.

- avoid bumping into objects.

- carry out simple, two-step directions: "Come to Daddy and bring your book"; express desires; ask questions.

- point to and name familiar objects; use two- or three-word sentences.

- enjoy being read to.

- show interest in playing with other children: watching, perhaps imitating.

- indicate a beginning interest in toilet training.

- sort familiar objects according to a single characteristic, such as type, color, or size.

Child's Name _____   Age _____
Observer _____   Date _____

Developmental Checklist (by four years)

Does the child . . .	Yes	No	Sometimes
1. Walk on a line?	☐	☐	☐
2. Balance on one foot briefly? Hop on one foot?	☐	☐	☐
3. Jump over an object 6 inches high and land on both feet together?	☐	☐	☐
4. Throw ball with direction?	☐	☐	☐
5. Copy circles and X's?	☐	☐	☐
6. Match six colors?	☐	☐	☐
7. Count to five?	☐	☐	☐
8. Pour well from pitcher? Spread butter, jam with knife?	☐	☐	☐
9. Button, unbutton large buttons?	☐	☐	☐
10. Know own sex, age, last name?	☐	☐	☐
11. Use toilet independently and reliably?	☐	☐	☐
12. Wash and dry hands unassisted?	☐	☐	☐
13. Listen to stories for at least five minutes?	☐	☐	☐
14. Draw head of person and at least one other body part?	☐	☐	☐
15. Play with other children?	☐	☐	☐
16. Share, take turns (with some assistance)?	☐	☐	☐
17. Engage in dramatic and pretend play?	☐	☐	☐
18. Respond appropriately to "Put it beside," "Put it under"?	☐	☐	☐
19. Respond to two-step directions: "Give me the sweater and put the shoe on the floor"?	☐	☐	☐
20. Respond by selecting the correct object—for example, hard versus soft object?	☐	☐	☐

Developmental Checklist, continued			
Does the child . . .	Yes	No	Sometimes
21. Answer "if," "what," and "when" questions?	☐	☐	☐
22. Answer questions about function: "What are books for"?	☐	☐	☐

DEVELOPMENTAL ALERTS

Check with a health care provider or early childhood specialist if, by the *fourth* birthday, the child *does not*

- have intelligible speech most of the time; have children's hearing checked if there is any reason for concern.

- understand and follow simple commands and directions.

- state own name and age.

- enjoy playing near or with other children.

- use three- to four-word sentences.

- ask questions.

- stay with an activity for three or four minutes; play alone several minutes at a time.

- jump in place without falling.

- balance on one foot, at least briefly.

- help with dressing self.

FIVE- TO SEVEN-YEAR-OLDS

- More independent of parents, able to take care of their own physical needs

- Rely upon their peer group for self-esteem, have two or three best friends

- Learn to share and take turns, participate in group games

- Are eager to learn and succeed in school

- Have a sense of duty and develop a conscience

- Are less aggressive and resolve conflicts with words

- Begin to see others' point of view

- Can sustain interest for long periods of time
- Can remember and relate past events
- Have good muscle control and can manage simple tools
- Have a high energy level

Child's Name _____   Age _____

Observer _____   Date _____

Developmental Checklist (by five years)

Does the child . . .	Yes	No	Sometimes
1. Walk backward, heel to toe?	☐	☐	☐
2. Walk up and down stairs, alternating feet?	☐	☐	☐
3. Cut on line?	☐	☐	☐
4. Print some letters?	☐	☐	☐
5. Point to and name three shapes?	☐	☐	☐
6. Group common related objects: shoe, sock, and foot; apple, orange, and plum?	☐	☐	☐
7. Demonstrate number concepts to four or five?	☐	☐	☐
8. Cut food with a knife: celery, sandwich?	☐	☐	☐
9. Lace shoes?	☐	☐	☐
10. Read from story picture book—in other words, tell story by looking at pictures?	☐	☐	☐
11. Draw a person with three to six body parts?	☐	☐	☐
12. Play and interact with other children; engage in dramatic play that is close to reality?	☐	☐	☐
13. Build complex structures with blocks or other building materials?	☐	☐	☐
14. Respond to simple three-step directions: "Give me the pencil, put the book on the table, and hold the comb in your hand"?	☐	☐	☐
15. Respond correctly when asked to show penny, nickel, and dime?	☐	☐	☐
16. Ask "How" questions?	☐	☐	☐
17. Respond verbally to "Hi" and "How are you"?	☐	☐	☐
18. Tell about event using past and future tenses?	☐	☐	☐
19. Use conjunctions to string words and phrases together—for example,"I saw a bear and a zebra and a giraffe at the zoo"?	☐	☐	☐

DEVELOPMENTAL ALERTS

Check with a health care provider or early childhood specialist if, by the *fifth* birthday, the child *does not*

- state own name in full.

- recognize simple shapes: circle, square, triangle.

- catch a large ball when bounced (have child's vision checked).

- speak so as to be understood by strangers (have child's hearing checked).

- have good control of posture and movement.

- hop on one foot.

- appear interested in, and responsive to, surroundings.

- respond to statements without constantly asking to have them repeated.

- dress self with minimal adult assistance; manage buttons, zippers.

- take care of own toilet needs; have good bowel and bladder control with infrequent accidents.

Child's Name _____   Age _____

Observer _____   Date _____

Developmental Checklist (by six years)

Does the child ...	Yes	No	Sometimes
1. Walk across a balance beam?	☐	☐	☐
2. Skip with alternating feet?	☐	☐	☐
3. Hop for several seconds on one foot?	☐	☐	☐
4. Cut out simple shapes?	☐	☐	☐
5. Copy own first name?	☐	☐	☐
6. Show well-established handedness; demonstrate consistent right- or left-handedness?	☐	☐	☐
7. Sort objects on one or more dimensions: color, shape, or function?	☐	☐	☐
8. Name most letters and numerals?	☐	☐	☐
9. Count by rote to 10; know what number comes next?	☐	☐	☐

Developmental Checklist, continued			
Does the child ...	Yes	No	Sometimes
10. Dress self completely; tie bows?	☐	☐	☐
11. Brush teeth unassisted?	☐	☐	☐
12. Have some concept of clock time in relation to daily schedule?	☐	☐	☐
13. Cross street safely?	☐	☐	☐
14. Draw a person with head, trunk, legs, arms, and features; often add clothing details?	☐	☐	☐
15. Play simple board games?	☐	☐	☐
16. Engage in cooperative play with other children, involving group decisions, role assignments, rule observance?	☐	☐	☐
17. Use construction toys, such as Legos, blocks, to make recognizable structures?	☐	☐	☐
18. Do 15-piece puzzles?	☐	☐	☐
19. Use all grammatical structures: pronouns, plurals, verb tenses, conjunctions?	☐	☐	☐
20. Use complex sentences: carry on conversations?	☐	☐	☐

DEVELOPMENTAL ALERTS

Check with a health care provider or early childhood specialist if, by the *sixth* birthday, the child *does not*

- alternate feet when walking up and down stairs.

- speak in a moderate voice; neither too loud, too soft, too high, too low.

- follow simple directions in stated order: "Please go to the cupboard, get a cup, and bring it to me."

- use four to five words in acceptable sentence structure.

- cut on a line with scissors.

- sit still and listen to an entire short story (five to seven minutes).

- maintain eye contact when spoken to (unless this is a cultural taboo).

- play well with other children.

- perform most self-grooming tasks independently: brush teeth, wash hands and face.

Child's Name _____   Age _____
Observer _____   Date _____

Developmental Checklist (by seven years)

Does the child . . .	Yes	No	Sometimes
1. Concentrate on completing puzzles and board games?	☐	☐	☐
2. Ask many questions?	☐	☐	☐
3. Use correct verb tenses, word order, and sentence structure in conversation?	☐	☐	☐
4. Correctly identify right and left hands?	☐	☐	☐
5. Make friends easily?	☐	☐	☐
6. Show some control of anger, using words instead of physical aggression?	☐	☐	☐
7. Participate in play that requires teamwork and rule observance?	☐	☐	☐
8. Seek adult approval for efforts?	☐	☐	☐
9. Enjoy reading and being read to?	☐	☐	☐
10. Use pencil to write words and numbers?	☐	☐	☐
11. Sleep undisturbed through the night?	☐	☐	☐
12. Catch a tennis ball, walk across a balance beam, hit a ball with a bat?	☐	☐	☐
13. Plan and carry out simple projects with minimal adult help?	☐	☐	☐
14. Tie own shoes?	☐	☐	☐
15. Draw pictures with greater detail and sense of proportion?	☐	☐	☐
16. Care for own personal needs with some adult supervision? Wash hands? Brush teeth? Use toilet? Dress self?	☐	☐	☐
17. Show some understanding of cause-and-effect concepts?	☐	☐	☐

DEVELOPMENTAL ALERTS

Check with a health care provider or early childhood specialist if, by the *seventh* birthday, the child *does not*

- show signs of ongoing growth, including increasing height and weight and continuing motor development, such as running, jumping, balancing.

- show some interest in reading and trying to reproduce letters, especially own name.

- follow simple, multiple-step directions: "Finish your book, put it on the shelf, and then get your coat on."

- follow through with instructions and complete simple tasks: putting dishes in the sink, picking up clothes, finishing a puzzle. (*Note:* All children forget. Task incompletion is not a problem unless a child *repeatedly* leaves tasks unfinished.)

- begin to develop alternatives to excessive use of inappropriate behaviors in order to get own way.

- develop a steady decrease in tension-type behaviors that may have developed with starting school: repeated grimacing or facial tics, eye twitching, grinding teeth, regressive soiling or wetting, frequent stomachaches, refusing to go to school.

8- TO 10-YEAR-OLDS

- Need parental guidance and support for school achievement.

- Competition is common.

- Pronounced gender differences in interests; same gender cliques formed.

- Spend a lot of time in physical game playing.

- Academic achievement is important.

- Begin to develop moral values, make value judgments about own behavior.

- Are aware of the importance of belonging.

- Strong gender role conformation.

- Begin to think logically and to understand cause and effect.

- Use language to communicate ideas and can use abstract words.

- Can read, but ability varies.

- Realize importance of physical skills in determining status among peers.

Child's Name _____   Age _____
Observer _____   Date _____

Developmental Checklist (by eight and nine years)

Does the child ...	Yes	No	Sometimes
1. Have energy to play, continuing growth, few illnesses?	☐	☐	☐
2. Use pencil in a deliberate and controlled manner?	☐	☐	☐
3. Express relatively complex thoughts in a clear and logical fashion?	☐	☐	☐
4. Carry out multiple four- to five-step instructions?	☐	☐	☐
5. Become less easily frustrated with own performance?	☐	☐	☐
6. Interact and play cooperatively with other children?	☐	☐	☐
7. Show interest in creative expression—telling stories, telling jokes, writing, drawing, singing?	☐	☐	☐
8. Use eating utensils with ease?	☐	☐	☐
9. Have a good appetite? Show interest in trying new foods?	☐	☐	☐
10. Know how to tell time?	☐	☐	☐
11. Have control of bowel and bladder functions?	☐	☐	☐
12. Participate in some group activities—games, sports, plays?	☐	☐	☐
13. Want to go to school? Seem disappointed if must miss a day?	☐	☐	☐
14. Demonstrate beginning skills in reading, writing, and math?	☐	☐	☐
15. Accept responsibility and complete work independently?	☐	☐	☐
16. Handle stressful situations without becoming overly upset?	☐	☐	☐

DEVELOPMENTAL ALERTS

Check with a health care provider or early childhood specialist if, by the *eighth* birthday, the child *does not*

- attend to the task at hand; show longer periods of sitting quietly, listening, responding appropriately.

- follow through on simple instructions.

- go to school willingly most days (of concern are excessive complaints about stomachaches or headaches when getting ready for school).

- make friends (observe closely to see if the child plays alone most of the time or withdraws consistently from contact with other children).

- sleep soundly most nights (frequent and recurring nightmares or bad dreams are usually at a minimum at this age).

- seem to see or hear adequately at times (squints, rubs eyes excessively, asks frequently to have things repeated).

- handle stressful situations without undue emotional upset (excessive crying, sleeping or eating disturbances, withdrawal, frequent anxiety).

- assume responsibility for personal care (dressing, bathing, feeding self) most of the time.

- show improved motor skills.

DEVELOPMENTAL ALERTS

Check with a health care provider or early childhood specialist if, by the *ninth* birthday, the child *does not*

- exhibit a good appetite and continued weight gain (some children, especially girls, may already begin to show early signs of an eating disorder).

- experience fewer illnesses.

- show improved motor skills, in terms of agility, speed, and balance.

- understand abstract concepts and use complex thought processes to problem-solve.

- enjoy school and the challenge of learning.

- follow through on multiple-step instructions.

- express ideas clearly and fluently.

- form friendships with other children and enjoy participating in group activities.

ELEVEN- TO THIRTEEN-YEAR-OLDS

■ Parental influence is decreasing and some rebellion may occur.

■ Peer group is important and sets standards for behavior.

■ Worry about what others think.

■ Choose friends based on common interests.

■ Gender differences in interests.

■ Develop awareness and interest in opposite gender.

■ Begin to question adult authority.

■ Often reluctant to attend child care; are bored or think they can care for themselves.

■ May be moody and experience stress over physical changes of puberty.

■ May be rebellious as they seek their own identity.

■ Can think abstractly and apply logic to solving problems.

■ Have a good command of spoken and written language.

■ Develop gender characteristics (girls); begin a growth spurt (boys).

■ Early maturing is related to a positive self-image.

■ Able to master physical skills necessary for playing games.

Child's Name _____   Age _____
Observer _____   Date _____

Developmental Checklist (by 10 and 11 years)

Does the child . . .	Yes	No	Sometimes
1. Continue to increase in height and weight?	☐	☐	☐
2. Exhibit improving coordination: running, climbing, riding a bike, writing?	☐	☐	☐
3. Handle stressful situations without becoming overly upset or violent?	☐	☐	☐

Developmental Checklist, continued

Does the child . . .	Yes	No	Sometimes
4. Construct sentences using reasonably correct grammar: nouns, adverbs, verbs, adjectives?	☐	☐	☐
5. Understand concepts of time, distance, space, volume?	☐	☐	☐
6. Have one or two "best friends"?	☐	☐	☐
7. Maintain friendships over time?	☐	☐	☐
8. Approach challenges with a reasonable degree of self-confidence?	☐	☐	☐
9. Play cooperatively and follow group instructions?	☐	☐	☐
10. Begin to show an understanding of moral standards: right from wrong, fairness, honesty, good from bad?	☐	☐	☐
11. Look forward to, and enjoy, school?	☐	☐	☐
12. Appear to hear well and listen attentively?	☐	☐	☐
13. Enjoy reasonably good health, with few episodes of illness or health-related complaints?	☐	☐	☐
14. Have a good appetite and enjoy mealtimes?	☐	☐	☐
15. Take care of own personal hygiene without assistance?	☐	☐	☐
16. Sleep through the night, waking up refreshed and energetic?	☐	☐	☐

DEVELOPMENTAL ALERTS

Check with a health care provider or early childhood specialist if, by the 11th birthday, the child *does not*

- continue to grow at a rate appropriate for the child's gender.

- show continued improvement of fine motor skills.

- make or keep friends.

- enjoy going to school and show interest in learning (have children's hearing and vision tested; vision and hearing problems affect children's ability to learn and their interest in learning).

- approach new situations with reasonable confidence.

- handle failure and frustration in a constructive manner.

- sleep through the night or experience prolonged problems with bedwetting, nightmares, or sleepwalking.

Child's Name _____   Age _____
Observer _____   Date _____

Developmental Checklist (by 12 and 13 years)

Does the child . . .	Yes	No	Sometimes
1. Appear to be growing: increasing height and maintaining a healthy weight (not too thin or too heavy)?	☐	☐	☐
2. Understand changes associated with puberty or have an opportunity to learn and ask questions?	☐	☐	☐
3. Complain of headaches or blurred vision?	☐	☐	☐
4. Have an abnormal posture or curving of the spine?	☐	☐	☐
5. Seem energetic and not chronically fatigued?	☐	☐	☐
6. Stay focused on a task and complete assignments?	☐	☐	☐
7. Remember and carry out complex instructions?	☐	☐	☐
8. Sequence, order, and classify objects?	☐	☐	☐
9. Use longer and more complex sentence structure?	☐	☐	☐
10. Engage in conversation; tell jokes and riddles?	☐	☐	☐
11. Enjoy playing organized games and team sports?	☐	☐	☐
12. Respond to anger-invoking situations without resorting to violence or physical aggression?	☐	☐	☐
13. Begin to understand and solve complex mathematical problems?	☐	☐	☐
14. Accept blame for actions on most occasions?	☐	☐	☐
15. Enjoy competition?	☐	☐	☐
16. Accept and carry out responsibility in a dependable manner?	☐	☐	☐
17. Go to bed willingly and wake up refreshed?	☐	☐	☐
18. Take pride in appearance; keep self reasonably clean?	☐	☐	☐

DEVELOPMENTAL ALERTS

Check with a health care provider or early childhood specialist if, by the *thirteenth* birthday, the child *does not*

- have movements that are smooth and coordinated.
- have energy sufficient for playing, riding bikes, or engaging in other desired activities.

- stay focused on tasks at hand.

- understand basic cause-and-effect relationships.

- handle criticism and frustration with a reasonable response (physical aggression and excessive crying could be an indication of other, underlying problems).

- exhibit a healthy appetite (frequent skipping of meals is not typical for this age group).

- make and keep friends.

Some content in this section adapted from Allen, E. A., and Marotz, L., *Developmental Profiles: Pre-birth through Twelve,* 4E, published by Thomson Delmar Learning.

As with the list of milestones by age, this list is not exhaustive, but it can be used to arrange an environment or to plan activities in your room.

BIRTH TO EIGHT YEARS

Cognitive	Date Observed
Recognizes familiar objects and people at a distance	
Starts using hands and eyes in coordination	
Finds partially hidden objects	
Explores objects in many different ways (shaking, banging, throwing, dropping)	
Finds hidden objects easily	
Imitates gestures	
Begins make-believe play	
Plays make-believe with dolls, animals, and people	
Recalls parts of a story	
Engages in fantasy play	
Language	
Smiles at the sound of voice	
Makes cooing noises; engages in vocal play	
Distinguishes emotions by tone of voice	
Responds to sound by making sounds	
Uses voice to express joy and displeasure	
Syllable repetition begins	
Makes simple gestures such as shaking head for no	
Babbles with inflection	
Uses exclamations such as "Uh-oh"	
Tells stories	
Social/Emotional	
Begins to develop a social smile	
Enjoys playing with other people and may cry when playing stops	
Becomes more communicative and expressive with face and body	

Social/Emotional, continued	Date Observed
Imitates some movements and facial expressions	
Enjoys social play	
Interested in mirror images	
Responds to other people's expression of emotion	
Enjoys imitating people in his or her play	
Repeats sounds or gestures for attention	
Imitates behavior of others, especially adults and older children	
Expresses a wide range of emotions	
Is more inventive in fantasy play	
May have imaginary friends or see monsters	
Wants to please and be with friends	
Is more likely to agree to rules	
Likes to sing, dance, and act	
Physical	
Transfers objects from hand to hand	
Looks for toy beyond tracking range	
Tracks moving objects with ease	
Grasps objects dangling in front of him	
Looks for fallen toys	
Uses pincer grasp (grasp using thumb and index finger)	
Bangs two 1-inch cubes together	
Puts objects into container	
Takes objects out of container	
Pokes with index finger	
Tries to imitate scribbling	
Scribbles spontaneously	
Makes vertical, horizontal, circular strokes with pencil or crayon	
Copies square shapes	
Draws a person with two to four body parts	
Uses scissors	
Draws circles and squares	
Begins to copy some capital letters	
Copies triangle and other geometric patterns	
Draws person with body	
Prints some letters	

9 TO 13 YEARS

Cognitive	Date Observed
Capable of sustained interest	
Begins to think logically	
Begins to understand cause and effect	
Understands abstract concepts	
Applies logic and solves problems	
Considers more than one solution to problems	
Enjoys problem solving games and puzzles	
Language	
Uses language to communicate ideas	
Uses language to express feelings	
Uses abstract words	
Often resorts to slang and profanity	
Often argumentative and contradicts adults	
Social/Emotional	
Sensitive to criticism	
Looks for friendly relationships with adults	
Makes value judgments about their own behavior	
Aware of the importance of belonging	
Exhibits strong conformation to gender role	
Independent and self-sufficient	
Begins to develop a moral values system	
May experience stress due to physical changes	
Seeks self-identity	
Physical	
High energy level	
Begins adolescent growth spurt (girls)	
Follows with a growth spurt (boys)	
Early maturing related to positive self-image	
Improved motor development and coordination (boys)	
Masters skills necessary for playing games (boys and girls)	

PLAY MATERIALS FOR CHILDREN

Children construct their own understanding of the world around them as they interact with appropriate materials and with other people. Very young children cannot learn through words alone. They do not learn best from paper and pencil practice exercises. Instead, they learn best through high-quality, hands-on experiences that are imaginative, engaging, and language-rich. They also learn best when guided through these experiences by skilled, caring, thoughtful adults. Young children need opportunities to choose materials and activities. They need the chance to figure out how to use new materials. Learning is increased when they can talk with one another and with friendly, informed adults about what they are doing. They benefit from opportunities to try on new roles through dramatic play and shape new environments through constructive play. They also need to combine active, sensory, joyful experiences with times of reflection, focus, storytelling, and conversation.

Research, such as the long-term High/Scope Perry Preschool Curriculum Comparison Project, shows that children who experience play-based, active learning do as well and better on early school tests as their peers who experience more paper- and drill-based, passive learning. Moreover, children who learn through play and problem solving mediated by supportive adults continue to do better with life choices and life skills in their later school years and into adulthood than children who did not have the same opportunity to think things through for themselves during play-based learning. When teachers provide a wealth of play materials and advocate for a child's right to learn through play, they give children the tools to develop a deep understanding of concepts that forms the foundation of school success and of success in managing the challenges of life.

Teachers play an important role in providing choices of good-quality playthings that match children's developmental abilities and interests. When budgets are limited, teachers must be able to select toys and materials that provide optimum learning opportunities. Creative teachers learn how to "scrounge" for toys, and to make playthings out of recycled materials.

For more information on the importance of play-based learning for young children, visit these Web sites:

High/Scope Educational Research Foundation: http://www.highscope.org

National Network for Child Care: http://www.nncc.org

CRITERIA FOR SELECTING PLAY EQUIPMENT FOR YOUNG CHILDREN

A young child's playthings should be as free of detail as possible.

- Too much detail hampers a child's freedom to express himself or herself.

- "Unstructured" toys, which allow the imagination free rein, include blocks, construction sets, clay, sand, and paints.

A good plaything should stimulate children to do things for themselves.

- Equipment that makes the child a spectator may entertain but has little or no play value.

- Play equipment should encourage children to explore and create or offer dramatic play potential.

Young children need large, easily manipulated playthings.

- Toys too small can be frustrating because the child's undeveloped muscular coordination cannot handle smaller forms and shapes.

- A child's muscles develop through play, so equipment should allow for climbing and balancing.

The material of which a plaything is constructed has an important role in the play of the young child.

- Warmth and pleasurable touch are significant (wood and cloth are the most satisfactory materials).

- The plaything's durability is of utmost importance.

- Play materials must be sturdy; axles and wheels must be able to support a child's weight.

- Children hate to see their toys break.

- Some materials break readily, which makes them expensive.

The toy must "work."

- Be sure parts move correctly.

- Make sure maintenance will be easy.

A plaything's construction should be simple enough for a child to comprehend.

- This strengthens the child's understanding and experience of the world.

- Mechanics should be visible and easily grasped; small children will take playthings apart to see how they tick.

A plaything should encourage cooperative play.

- Provide an environment that stimulates children to work and play together.

The total usefulness of the plaything must be considered in comparing price.

- Will it last several children through several stages of their playing lives?

The lists that follow suggest the materials that are priorities for children at particular levels of development.

FOR YOUNG INFANTS BIRTH THROUGH SIX MONTHS

- unbreakable mirrors that can be attached low on walls or near changing tables and cribs

- stuffed, washable toys or rag dolls, with stitched faces and eyes

- mobiles and visuals hung out of reach

- grasping toys: simple rattles, squeeze toys, keys on ring, clutch or texture balls

- hanging toys for batting
- wrist or ankle bells

FOR OLDER, MOBILE INFANTS SEVEN THROUGH TWELVE MONTHS

- soft rubber animals for grasping
- simple one-piece vehicles 6–8 inches high, with large wheels
- grasping toys for skill development: toys on suction cups, stacking rings, nesting cups, squeeze toys, plastic pop beads, bean bags, busy boxes
- containers and objects to fill and dump
- small cloth, plastic, and board books
- soft cloth or foam blocks for stacking
- simple floating objects for water play
- balls of all kinds, including some with special effects
- low, soft climbing platforms
- large unbreakable mirrors
- infant swings for outdoors
- recorded music and songs

FOR TODDLERS ONE TO THREE YEARS

For Fine Motor Skills

- nesting materials
- sand and water play toys: funnels, colanders, small sand tools
- simple activity boxes, with doors, lids, switches, more complex after about 18 months: turning knob or key
- pegboards with large pegs
- four- or five-piece stacking materials
- pop beads and stringing beads
- simple three- to five-piece puzzles with knobs, familiar shapes

- simple matching materials
- books, including tactile books, cloth, plastic, and board picture books

For Gross Motor Skills

- push and pull toys
- simple doll carriages and wagons
- stable riding toys with four wheels and no pedals
- balls of all sizes
- tunnels for crawling through
- tumbling mats and low climbing platforms

For Pretend Play

- small wood or plastic people and animal figures
- small cars and trucks
- dolls
- plastic dishes and pots and pans
- doll beds
- hats
- simple dress-ups
- telephones
- scarves and fabrics

For Sensory Play

- recorded music and player
- play dough
- fingerpaint
- large nontoxic crayons
- sturdy paper
- simple musical instruments

FOR CHILDREN THREE THROUGH FIVE

For Gross Motor Play

- small wagons and wheelbarrows

- replications of adult tools for pushing and pretend play, such as lawn mower, shopping cart

- scooters

- tricycles and other vehicles with steering ability

- riding toys for more than one child

- balls of all sizes, especially 10-inch and 12-inch balls for kicking and throwing

- hollow plastic bat and lightweight ball

- jump rope

- stationary outdoor climbing equipment

- slides and ladders

- outdoor building materials, tires, and other loose parts

Exploration and Mastery Play Materials

- sand and water play: measures, funnels, tubes, sand tools

- construction materials: unit blocks, large hollow blocks

- Lego-type plastic interlocking blocks

- puzzles, including fit-in puzzles and large, simple jigsaw puzzles, with varying numbers of pieces, according to children's age

- pattern-making materials: beads for stringing, pegboards, mosaic boards, feltboards, color cubes

- dressing, lacing, and stringing: sewing cards and dressing frames

- collections of small plastic objects for matching, sorting, and ordering by color, shape, size, or other category concepts

- simple, concrete number materials for counting and matching to numerals

- measuring materials: scales, measuring cups for liquids

- science materials: magnifying glass, color paddles, objects from the natural world, including pets

- beginning computer programs

- games: dominoes; lotto games; bingo by color, number, or picture; first board games that use concepts such as color or counting; memory

- books of all kinds: picture books, realistic stories, alphabet picture books, poetry, information books

- writing center materials: clipboards, colored pencils, old calendars, envelopes, notepads, stationery, rubber stamps and ink pads, rulers, magnetic letters, stencil shapes, stickers, file cards, and office materials

For Pretend Play

- dolls of various ethnic and gender appearance, with clothes and other accessories and furniture

- housekeeping equipment

- variety of dress-ups, including those related to various roles and themes

- transportation toys

- hand puppets

- animal and human figures for play scenes

- full-length, unbreakable mirror

For Creative Play

- art and craft materials: crayons, markers, easel, paintbrushes, paint and fingerpaint, varieties of paper, chalkboard and chalk, safety scissors, glue, collage materials, clay and play dough, and tools to use with them

- workbench with hammer, saw, and nails

- musical instruments

- recorded music for singing, movement and dancing, listening, and for using with rhythm instruments

FOR CHILDREN SIX THROUGH EIGHT YEARS

For Gross Motor Play

- balls and sports equipment for beginning team play, such as soccer, baseball

- complex climbing structures: ropes, ladders, rings, hanging bars

- materials for target practice

- mats for acrobatics

- bicycles and scooters

For Exploration and Mastery Play

- construction materials for large constructions and for creating models, including metal parts and nuts and bolts

- puzzles: 100-piece jigsaw puzzles, three-dimensional puzzles such as Rubik's cubes

- craft materials for braiding, weaving, knitting, leather craft, jewelry making, sewing

- pattern-making materials: mosaic tiles, geometric puzzles

- games: word games, simple card games, reading and spelling games, number and counting games, beginning strategy games such as checkers

- materials for specific learning: printing materials, math manipulatives, measuring materials, science materials, and computer programs for language arts, number and concept development, and for problem solving activities

- books at a variety of levels for beginning readers—see the Resources list on page 86.

For Creative Activities

- variety of markers, colored pencils, chalks, paintbrushes and paints, art papers for tracing and drawing

- clay and tools, including pottery wheel

- workbench with wood and variety of tools

- real instruments such as guitars and recorders

- music for singing and movement

- audiovisual materials for independent use

Some ideas adapted from Bronson, M., *The Right Stuff for Children Birth to 8: Selecting Play Materials to Support Development*, published by the National Association for the Education of Young Children.

Free and Low-Cost Play Materials

Remember that recycled materials and other loose parts have many uses for exploration and creativity. These materials can be valuable tools in a number of curriculum areas:

- Empty plastic containers: detergent bottles, bleach bottles, old refrigerator containers, which can be used for constructing scoops, storing art materials, and so on.

- Buttons—all colors and sizes—are excellent for collages, assemblages, as well as sorting, counting, matching, and so on.

- Egg shells, which can be washed, dried, and colored with food coloring for art projects.

- Coffee or shortening cans and lids, which can be covered with adhesive paper and used for storage of art supplies, games, and manipulatives materials.

- Magazines with colorful pictures, which are excellent for making collages, murals, and posters.

- Scraps of fabric: felt, silk, cotton, oil cloth, and so on, which can be used to make "fabric boards" with the name of each fabric written under a small swatch attached to the board, as well as for collages, puppets, and more.

- Yarn scraps, which can be used for separating buttons into sets; also for art activities.

- Styrofoam scraps.

- Scraps of lace, rick rack, or decorative trim.

- Bottles with sprinkler tops, which are excellent for water play and for mixing water as children fingerpaint.

- Wallpaper books of discontinued patterns.

- Paper doilies.

- Discarded wrapping paper.

- Paint color cards from paint/hardware stores.

- Old paintbrushes.

- Old jewelry and beads.

- Old muffin tins, which are effective for sorting small objects and mixing paint.

- Tongue depressors or ice cream sticks, which can be used as counters for math and are good for art construction projects, stick puppets, and so on.

- Wooden clothespins, which can be used for making "people," for construction projects, and for hanging up paintings to dry.

Adapted from Mayesky, M., *Creative Activities for Young Children*, 7E, published by Thomson Delmar Learning.

BASIC PROGRAM EQUIPMENT AND MATERIALS FOR AN EARLY CHILDHOOD CENTER

If you are responsible for ordering supplies for your classroom or early childhood program, the following guidelines will be useful.

INDOOR EQUIPMENT

The early childhood room should be arranged into well-planned areas of interest, such as the housekeeping and doll corner, block building area, and so on to encourage children to play in small groups throughout the playroom, engaging in activities of their special interest, rather than attempting to play in one large group.

The early childhood center must provide selections of indoor play equipment from many areas of interest. Selection should be of sufficient quantities so that children can participate in a wide range of activities. Many pieces of equipment can be homemade. Consider the age and developmental levels of the children when making selections.

Playroom Furnishings

- *Tables:* seat four to six children (18 inches high for three-year-olds, 20–22-inches high for four- and five-year-olds)

- *Chairs:* 10 inches high for three-year-olds, 12–14 inches high for four- and five-year-olds

- *Open shelves:* 26 inches high, 12 inches deep, 12 inches between shelves

- *Lockers:* 12 inches wide, 12 inches deep, 32–36 inches high

Housekeeping or Doll Corner

Item	Number Recommended for 10 Children
Dolls	3
Doll clothes	Variety
Doll bed—should be large enough for a child to get into, bedding	1
Doll high chair	1
Small table, four chairs	1 set
Tea party dishes	6-piece set with tray
Stove: child size, approximately 24 × 23 × 12 inches	1
Sink: child size, approximately 24 × 23 × 12 inches	1
Refrigerator: child size, approximately 28 × 23 × 12 inches	1
Pots and pans, empty food cartons, measuring cups, spoons, and so on	Variety
Mop, broom, dustpan	1
Ironing board and iron	1
Clothespins and clothesline	1
Toy telephones	2
Dress-up box—men's and women's hats, neckties, pocketbooks, shoes, old dresses, scarves, jewelry, and so on	Variety
Mirror	1

Art Supplies

Item	Number Recommended for 10 Children
Newsprint paper 18 × 24 inches	1 ream
Colored paper—variety	3 packages
Large crayons	10 boxes
Tempera paint—red, yellow, blue, black, white	1 can each
Long-handled paintbrushes: making a stroke from ½ inch to 1 inch wide	10–12
Easels	1
Fingerpaint paper: glazed paper such as shelf, freezer, or butcher's paper	1 roll
Paste	1 quart
Blunt scissors	10
Collage: collection of bits of colored paper, cut-up gift wrappings, ribbons, cotton, string, scraps of fabric, and so on for pasting	Variety
Magazines for cutting and pasting	Variety

Item, continued	Number Recommended for 10 Children
Clay: play dough	50 pounds
Cookie cutters, rolling pins	Variety
Smocks or aprons to protect children's clothes	10

Block Building Area

Item	Number Recommended for 10 Children
Unit blocks: purchased	276 pieces, 11 shapes
Large, lightweight blocks	Variety
Small wooden or rubber animals and people	Variety
Small trucks, airplanes, cars, and boats	12
Medium airplanes	3
Medium boats	2
Medium-sized trucks: 12 to 24 inches	3

Music Corner

- record player, tape player, CD player
- suitable records, tapes, and CDs
- rhythm instruments
- dress-up scarves for dancing

Manipulative Toys

Item	Number Recommended for 10 Children
Wooden inlay puzzles, approximately 5 to 20 pieces	6
Color cone	1
Nested blocks	1
Pegboards, variety of shapes and sizes	1
Large spools and beads for stringing	2 sets
Toys that have parts that fit into one another	2
Lotto games	2
Dominoes	1

Books and Stories

A carefully selected book collection (20–30 books) for the various age levels should include the following:

- transportation, birds and animals, family life
- community helpers, science, nonsense rhymes
- Mother Goose rhymes, poems, and stories
- homemade picture books
- collection of pictures classified by subject
- library books to enrich the collection

Nature Study and Science

- aquarium or fish bowls
- plastic materials
- magnifying glass, prism, magnet, thermometers
- growing indoor plants, garden plot
- stones, leaves, acorns, birds' nests, caterpillars, worms, tadpoles, and so on

Woodworking Center

Basic woodworking operations are

- sanding
- gluing
- hammering
- holding (with a vise or clamp)
- fastening (with screws)
- drilling
- sawing

Materials for a woodworking center include the following:

- sturdy workbench (or table)
- woodworking tools: broad-headed nails ¾ to 1½ inches long; C-clamp or vise (to hold wood); flat-headed, 12-oz. hammer for beginning woodworking experiences, later a

claw hammer may be added; 14-inch saw with 10 teeth to the inch

- soft white pine lumber scraps (it is difficult to drive nails into hardwood; plywood is not suitable either); packing boxes of soft pine can be disassembled and used for hammering work

Sand Play

- For outdoors, sand should be confined so it is not scattered over the rest of the playground.

- Outdoor area should be large enough for several children to move about without crowding each other.

- A 10- to 12-inch ledge around a sandbox can serve as a boundary and provide children with a working surface or a seat.

- Keep sand to 6 to 8 inches below the top of the ledge so that it is less likely to spill out.

- Sand should be about 18 inches deep so children can dig or make tunnels.

- For drainage, include 4 or 5 inches of gravel on the bottom of the sandbox.

- Basic equipment: plastic or metal kitchen utensils, cups, spoons, pails, shovels, sifters, funnels, scoops, bowls.

Water Play

- Can be either indoor or outdoor activity, depending on climate.

- Can use clear plastic water basins on a stand with wheels to allow them to be moved to any area of a room.

- When using plastic basins, children can see through the sides and the bottom.

- For tables on a carpeted floor, use a plastic runner to protect the carpet.

- Materials: Clear tubing, sponges, strainers, funnels, corks, pitchers, and measuring cups; for added interest: rotary beaters, spoons, small bowls, plastic basters, and straws.

OUTDOOR EQUIPMENT

Outdoor play equipment should be grouped according to use. For example, plan for both active and quiet play; allow for free areas for use of wheel toys. Suggested basic outdoor play equipment for the early childhood program includes the following:

- climbing structure(s)
- large and small packing boxes
- slides
- swings with canvas seats
- wagons and wheelbarrows
- pedal toys: tricycles, cars, and so on
- sandbox with spoons, shovels, pails, and so on
- balls
- a variety of salvage materials: rubber tires, tire tubes, lengths of garden hose, ropes, and cardboard boxes

Note: Many activities, such as housekeeping play and art activities, at times can be transferred to the outdoor area.

Use this checklist to evaluate your playground setup:

☐ Pathways are clear and spacious enough between areas so that traffic flows well and equipment does not obstruct the children's movement.

☐ Space and equipment are organized so that children are readily visible and easily supervised by adults.

☐ Different activity areas are separated. (Tricycle paths are separate from the swings; the sandbox is separate from the climbing area.)

☐ Open space is available for active play.

☐ Some space is available for quiet play.

☐ Dramatic play can be set up outdoors, as space is available.

☐ Art activities can be set up outdoors.

☐ A portion of the play area is covered for use in wet weather.

☐ A storage area is available for play equipment.

☐ A drinking fountain is available.

☐ The area has readily accessible restrooms.

For more information on play equipment and materials go to these Web sites:

http://www.kaplanco.com

http://www.eichild.com

http://www.lakeshorelearning.com/

http://www.montessoriland.com/

http://www.bellalunatoys.com/

http://www.turnthepage.com

OBSERVATION AND ASSESSMENT

A variety of tools can be used to assess children's development. Using assessment tools in conjunction with developmental milestones helps caregivers recognize a child's developmental accomplishments as well as determine the child's next growth steps. The teacher needs to observe each child to determine the level to which each child is performing independently so that instruction can begin. This knowledge is useful in planning curriculum, designing the room environment for success, and establishing appropriate techniques that help children manage their own behavior. No doubt your college practicum experience taught you the logistics of observing: using objective descriptions and recording specific, dated, brief, and factual information. Observation can take many forms:

■ anecdotal records

■ running records

■ checklists

■ time or event sampling

Anecdotal records are brief notes kept by the teacher while the child is performing a task. At first, this may seem daunting, but it will become part of your everyday routine. Keep a small spiral notebook and pen or pencil in your pocket. When a child begins an activity, watch what the child does and write down three or four things that you actually observe the child doing. Remember the facts and only the facts. For example:

Johnny H. picks up handful of clay at the art center. Shapes clay into bird. Talks with teacher. Saves clay bird on craft shelf.

As time permits, probably during nap time, the brief notes are turned into a full scenario so that anyone could read the record at a later date:

ANECDOTAL RECORD

Child's Name: Johnny H.

Observer's Name: Jorge

Age: 7 yr. 5 mo.

Date: April 27, 2005

What actually happened/What I saw	Developmental Interpretation (Select 1 or 2 of the following)	
Johnny H. went to the clay center for the third time this week. He picked up a handful of clay and shaped it into a bird that fit in his hand. He worked on the bird for 15 minutes and did not look up during that time. He used a pointed stick to mark eyes and detailed feathers on the bird. He stepped back from the table, turned to face his teacher and said, "I made this for my mum's birthday. Can I save it?" His teacher said, "I think she will really like that Johnny. Sure you can save it." Johnny carried the bird over to the craft shelf using both hands and then cleaned up his work space at the clay table.	Interest in learning	
	Self-esteem/self-concept	
	Cultural acceptance	
	Problem solving	
	Interest in real-life mathematical concepts	
	Interactions with adults	
	Literacy	
	Interactions with peers	
	Language expression/comprehension	
	Self-regulation	
	Safe/healthy behavior	
	Self-help skills	
	Gross motor skills	
	Fine motor skills	

ANECDOTAL RECORD

Child's Name: _____   Date: _____
Observer's Name: _____

What actually happened/What I saw	Developmental Interpretation (Select 1 or 2 of the following)	
	Interest in learning	
	Self-esteem/self-concept	
	Cultural acceptance	
	Problem solving	
	Interest in real-life mathematical concepts	
	Interactions with adults	
	Literacy	
	Interactions with peers	
	Language expression/comprehension	
	Self-regulation	
	Safe/healthy behavior	
	Self-help skills	
	Gross motor skills	
	Fine motor skills	

RUNNING RECORD

Another form of authentic assessment is the running record, which covers a longer time span and gives more information than an anecdotal record. Often it may have a specific developmental focus such as "social interactions." A running record gives you information about other developmental areas because of its very detailed nature. This form of observation requires the caregiver not to be involved with children for several minutes while writing the observation. You will be setting yourself apart from the children and writing continuously, in as much detail as possible. You will write what the child does and says, by herself or himself and in interactions with other people and materials. Use objective phrases and avoid interpretative and judgmental language. Note that the format for this form of assessment has two columns. The left column is for writing the actual observations and the right column is for connecting the observations to aspects of development. Remember to date all observations so you can notice developmental change over time.

RUNNING RECORD

Child's Name: Trish H.   Age: 7 yr. 5 mo.
Observer's Name: Jorge   Date: April 27, 2005
Developmental Focus: Social Interactions with Peers

Trish H., Sonya J., and Mary P. mark a hopscotch pattern on the playground. Trish, Sonya, and Mary take turns and reach space number 4. Trish and Sonya chant, "Mary Mack" as Mary hops. Mary hops on a line. Trish gives Mary a side hug as Mary steps to the side of the hopscotch area. Trish says, "Don't worry. I used to not be able to make that jump. You'll get it, too." Angie R. runs up and jumps onto the hopscotch grid. Sonya and Mary start to yell at her, "Hey, dummy, get out of our game!" Trish puts her hands by her sides. She stands by the grid and says, "Angie, if you want to join in, you can, but it's my turn next." Angie continues to jump around on the grid. Trish runs over to Shana (after-school co-teacher) and says, "Shana, could you please tell Angie to get in line for her turn? I already tried." Shana tells Angie to line up behind Sonya and Mary if she wants a turn. Angie does. Trish throws her stone inside square 5 and hops and jumps from square to square without touching any of the lines or falling over. She says, "Yeah, I got 5, only 3 more to go. I love this game. It feels like I'm dancing."	Participates in cooperative activities
	Early literacy/expressive language
	Expresses empathy
	Communicates knowledge of growing skills
	Self-regulation/controls emotions
	Stands up for own rights
	Asks for what she needs
	Gross motor skills
	Math skill
	Self-awareness

CHECKLIST

A checklist is often used as a means of assessment because it is one of the easiest assessment tools to use. A checklist consists of a pre-determined list of clearly observable developmental criteria for which the observer indicates "yes" or "no." The observer reads the developmental criteria and makes a checkmark if the decision is a "yes." This form of assessment requires that no additional notes be recorded. Many teachers design their own checklists to fit the specific needs of their program. The following checklist is an example of one that might be used to assess social skills of children.

SOCIAL SKILLS CHECKLIST

Child's Name: Age: yr.   mo.
Observer's Name:

Skills	Dates
■ Desires to and can work near other children	
■ Interacts with other children	
■ Takes turns with other children	
■ Enters play with others in positive manner	
■ Shares materials and supplies	
■ Stands up for own rights in positive manner	
■ Forms friendships with peers	
■ Engages in positive commentary on other children's work	
■ Shows empathy	
■ Negotiates compromises with other children	
■ Demonstrates prosocial behavior	
■ Participates in cooperative group activities	
■ Resolves conflicts with adult prompts	
■ Resolves conflicts without adult prompts	

Make checklists for each center in your classroom and hang them on clipboards. When you observe the children at play in each center, check off skills by placing a date in the appropriate box.

The last type of observation that a teacher should perform is a time or event sampling. These are similar in focus, but different, too. A **time sampling** asks the teacher to set a timer and each time the timer goes off, the teacher looks at a particular child and writes down what the child is doing. Again only the facts are written:

The timer is set to go off every 10 minutes. I will look at Johnny and see what he is doing when I hear the timer. The timer goes off, I look at Johnny. Johnny is standing under the shade tree looking in the direction of the ball game that three 10-year-old boys are playing. The timer goes off again. Johnny has a soft ball and is throwing it up and catching it on the edge of the hardtop surface, which is next to the ball game that five 9- and 10-year-old boys are playing.

As mentioned, an **event sampling** is similar, but the teacher looks at events instead of being directed by a timer. The teacher zeros in on an event and writes down all things that he or she sees pertaining to the event.

Event Sample

Antecedent	Behavior	Consequence
Cameron (21 months) is pushing a yellow truck across the floor, while making a low, "broom, broom" sound. Susan (teacher) is on the opposite side of the room washing her hands after changing a diaper. Nicky (19 months) runs toward Cameron, bends over, and pulls the truck out of Cameron's hand. Nicky twists away from Cameron.	Cameron stands up, screams so loudly that everyone in the room looks up; Cameron bends toward Nicky and bites Nicky's right shoulder.	Nicky and Cameron both begin to cry. Nicky hugs the truck tighter. Susan walks quickly to Nicky. She puts her hand on his arm and says, "Ouch, Nicky. That must have hurt. Biting hurts. Let's check your shoulder and get some ice to put on it." Then she turns to Cameron and tells him, "No biting, Cameron. Biting hurts. Say a big 'No! No!' to Nicky when he takes your truck. Come and help me put some ice on Nicky's hurt. Then we'll find another yellow truck."

Assessment and observation may seem overwhelming as you begin your career in early childhood. Do not shy away from them. Take the challenge and begin to look for the positive aspects of learning and mastering a new skill. Picture yourself as a student in your classroom and imagine what it is like to perfect something your teacher has just asked you to do. How does it make you feel? Now begin.

- You have the day planned for outdoor activities and there is an unexpected rainstorm. What will you do?

- It is your day off and you get a call at the last minute to cover for a co-worker who is ill. You find out that nothing has been planned. What activities can you implement quickly?

- You were promised that the materials you needed for your planned art activity would be on site when you arrived at work, but there was a shipping delay and they aren't there. What is an alternative activity you can easily set up and implement?

Being prepared at all times with a few backup activities will make your job much less stressful. Some of the activities listed here require only a few materials that you might want to have on hand at all times.

TITLE OF ACTIVITY: ROLL THE BALL

Developmental Focus: Social/Emotional (Interpersonal Intelligence)

Goal: Infants will interact with adult caregiver in turn-taking by rolling ball back and forth and engaging in verbal and nonverbal dialogue centered on this activity.

Age Range: Older infants and one-year-olds

Materials: Three to four brightly colored balls, including balls with interesting features such as an object inside a clear ball, a glittery ball, and so on

Procedure:

- Ensure that the children are well rested, well fed, comfortable, alert, and ready for interactive play.

- Invite the children to the floor play area by holding the balls up and talking about the balls. Use invitation words such as "come" and "see." Wonder aloud what the balls can do as you gather the children at the floor play area.

- Sit with your legs open close to the children and roll a ball to a child who is looking at the ball. Talk about what you are doing and what the child does in response.

- Continue with the activity, changing balls when needed to stimulate the children's interest and showing the children how to push the balls as needed. Be sure to talk about what you are doing, what the children are doing, and to expand on what they say. Example: Say "Benito is rolling the red ball. Go, Benito!"

- Close the activity as the children lose interest by saying, "We rolled balls." Name the individual children who rolled balls with you. Talk about what you are doing as you put the balls away.

- A great follow-up to this activity would be some lap and snuggle time during which you share a board book that features pictures of familiar objects including balls.

Note: This activity will also develop the children's cognitive and physical skills, but the focus will be on encouraging a warm, positive interaction with turn-taking.

Note to Administrators: Ensure that there is always a varied supply of clean, colorful, appropriate balls available for the infant and toddler classrooms.

TITLE OF ACTIVITY: BUBBLES

Developmental Focus: Cognitive, Physical (Logical-Mathematical, Bodily-Kinesthetic, and Naturalist Intelligences)

Goal: Children will track, blow, and count bubbles and move with bubbles.

Age Range: Infants–five years

Materials: Small plastic containers, bubble solution, and a variety of bubble "wands"

Procedure:

- Bring the children to an open area.

- For infants and toddlers who have not yet learned to blow bubbles, blow bubbles for them to track.

- For children who can blow bubbles independently, provide them with their own container and wand to blow bubbles.

- Count the bubbles with the children. Count in seconds how long they "last."

- Show children how they can make bubbles by moving the wand in an arc so that the air moves through the wand and "blows" the bubble.

- Play gentle music and do a bubble dance.

Note to Administrators: Bubbles are also a great teaching tool for developing self-control, vocabulary, and imagination. Keep a good supply on hand as they also create a "natural" experience with some of the spontaneous quality of outdoor activities on days when children cannot go outside.

TITLE OF ACTIVITY: LET'S MARCH!

Developmental Focus: Cognitive/Creative Expression, Physical (Musical, Spatial, and Bodily-Kinesthetic Intelligences)

Goal: Children will develop ideas to express themselves in sound, movement, color, and line.

Age Range: Two–five years

Materials: Musical instruments, drawing paper, large crayons

Procedure:

- Invite the children to the circle area.

- Introduce the musical instruments. Have multiple instruments of each type and no more than three types of instruments. Children take turns to choose an instrument.

- Teach a "stop and listen" signal to the children.

- Encourage the children to make noise with their instruments, then practice your "stop and listen" signal.

- Invite the children to follow you in a "marching band."

- March while making noise with the instruments, make loud noise, soft noise, march with the instruments held high, and march with the instruments held low. Practice the "stop and listen" signal as needed.

- Invite ideas from the children; for example, "How else could we march and play our instruments?" Build on ideas that you see/hear the children offering you.

- March with the children to the table area. Provide paper and crayons and invite the children to draw marching pictures. Have a container available for the children to place their instruments in as they move to drawing.

- Talk with the children about their drawing and the experience of marching with the musical instruments.

- A great opener or follow-up for this activity would be to read, *Crash, Bang, Boom* (board book version by Peter Spier, Doubleday, 1990).

- Instruments can be commercial or "homemade," such as paper plate tambourines. Gather a good supply of recycled materials for your program so that oatmeal boxes and other safe containers are always available. In the absence of any materials to use for instruments, children who have begun to pretend could also do this activity with imaginary instruments.

Note to Administrators: Provide a well-organized resource area with a variety of duplicated musical instruments and with recycled materials to make improvised instruments.

TITLE OF ACTIVITY: "MAGIC PICTURE" CRAYON RUBBINGS

Developmental Focus: Cognitive, Physical (Logical-Mathematical, Spatial, and Naturalist Intelligences)

Goals: Children will develop a greater awareness of their environment while developing fine motor skill.

Age Range: Four–six years

Materials: A variety of objects found in the early childhood class-room, newsprint, crayons

Procedure:

- At circle time, tell children that you know how to draw a "magic picture" of a pair of scissors and demonstrate how to make a crayon rubbing of the scissors.

- Explain that different pressures will get different results and that crayon rubbings work best with patience and persistence.

- Provide children with paper and crayons and a selection of objects suitable for making rubbings.

- Invite children to find other objects and surfaces in the room to use for crayon rubbings.

- Talk about the rubbings with the children as they work, discuss details that they notice and images that emerge in the process of completing the rubbings, and have children match objects with rubbings that have been completed.

- This activity can be extended outdoors with rubbings of leaves and other natural surfaces and with pencil rubbing as children gain more control.

Note to Administrators: Encourage all your teaching staff to see both the classroom and the outdoors as environments that are full of materials for learning and creativity, rather than relying solely on commercially produced materials.

TITLE OF THE ACTIVITY: INDOOR WEATHER

Developmental Focus: Cognitive/Creative (Spatial and Naturalist Intelligences)

Goal: Children will use a variety of materials to express their ideas about the weather.

Age Range: Four–six years

Materials: Construction paper, glue, cotton balls, markers, yarn, and newspaper

Procedure:

- On a rainy day, talk with the children about the weather outside.

- Provide the materials for the children to make "Indoor Weather" collages. Tell them they can make the collages rainy, snowy, sunny, or use other ideas that they may have.

- Invite children to tell you about their collages and record their thoughts on story dictation as time permits. Those who can write independently can do so.

- Close this activity by reading an old favorite, *Cloudy with a Chance of Meatballs* (by Judith Barrett illustrated by Ron Barrett, Macmillan, 1978) and see where it takes you.

Note to Administrators: Order basic art supplies such as construction paper, glue, and collage materials well in advance and establish a system to keep stocks well supplied so that teachers will always have materials available for both emergencies and emergent curriculum activities.

TITLE OF ACTIVITY: SILLY RHYMES SCAVENGER HUNT

Developmental Focus: Cognitive/Language (Linguistic and Logical-Mathematical Intelligences)

Goal: Children will develop increased phonological awareness as they explore rhymes and wordplay.

Age Range: Five–seven years

Materials: Everyday items from around the classroom

Procedure:

- Invite children to the circle area and have each child join with a partner.

- Tell children that they are going on a silly rhymes scavenger hunt to find objects in their classroom and give them a new silly name.

- Partners conduct a scavenger hunt around the room to find an object in a given category, for example, a red object, a round object, or a wooden object.

- Partners meet at the circle area with the object they have found.

- Draw a large consonant on the dry-erase board or chart paper.

- Instead of saying the name of the object, partners use the given consonant to rhyme with the object's name. For example, if the consonant is "S" and the object is a block, partners would say, "we found a sock," instead of, "we found a block."

- Close this activity by sharing a rhyming book such as *Sheep in a Jeep* (by Nancy E. Shaw illustrated by Margot Apple, Houghton-Mifflin, 1997).

Note to Administrators: Ensure that teaching staff and volunteers have the opportunity to learn activities such as rhyming games, syllable clapping, and so on to promote phonological awareness (awareness and understanding of sounds in their environment) to prepare children for phonemic awareness (letter–sound correspondences) as they begin to read.

TITLE OF ACTIVITY: "RAINBOW OF FEELINGS" COLLAGES

Developmental Focus: Social/Emotional, Cognitive/Creative Expression (Linguistic, Spatial, and Intrapersonal Intelligences)

Goal: Children will develop self-awareness and the ability to express and manage emotions in creative ways.

Age Range: Five years and up

Materials: Paper, a variety of appropriate full-color magazines, scissors, glue, markers

Procedure:

- Open with a discussion of chameleons. Discuss how they can change their color to blend in with their surroundings. They can be different colors at different times. Discuss how color can also reflect our internal feelings. Discuss what colors the children associate with different feelings.

- Provide the magazines and other materials and invite the children to select pictures by focusing on the color of the pictures to express the color of their feelings.

- Be available to talk with the children about their ideas, feelings, pictures they encounter, and so on.

- Invite children to talk about their collages and wrap up the activity by talking about how we can change our feelings and internal color, just as chameleons can change their color.

- A great opener or follow-up for this activity would be to read *The Mixed-Up Chameleon* (by Eric Carle, Harper Collins Children's Books, 1988).

Note to Administrators: As part of your resource area, work with staff and families to accumulate a collection of appropriate magazines that teachers will be able to use for a wide variety of activities for art, literacy, and so on.

A number of Web sites offer sample lesson plans for teachers. When downloading lesson plans from the Internet or another source, be sure each plan lists the

- objective or goal of the lesson.

- materials needed.

- directions for the activity.

- appropriate age group.

- developmental appropriateness.

Check the Resources section of this manual for a list of Web sites with lesson plans and other free materials for teachers.

BOOKS FOR CHILDREN

Reading aloud is a wonderful gift you can give to children. Through sharing an interesting book, you introduce them to a world they might not otherwise be able to visit. Through books, you can travel anywhere you like, have experiences outside the realm of your current environment, participate in wonderful fantasies, and be saddened and then uplifted.

Children's desire to read and the ability to do so is fostered by reading to them as soon as they are born. Even babies can enjoy looking at picture books and hearing simple stories. Preschoolers love to have favorite books read to them repeatedly. As children move into the school years, they can sustain their interest in longer books that are divided into chapters. When they realize the joy that comes from good books, they are more motivated to read on their own.

Many textbooks provide suggestions for setting up reading corners and providing books for children to read by themselves. This section focuses on books that you can read aloud to children in small or large groups. Remember that the more you read, the better you will become at doing so. When the books have been enjoyed in a group setting, add them to the book corner for children to read alone. In addition, teachers often create lending arrangements where children can take home books for their parents to read and then return. Teachers who believe in the importance of reading choose the best of children's literature and involve families in reading.

HOW TO GET CHILDREN TO LISTEN AND WANT MORE

- Schedule time each day for reading, maybe toward the end of the day when children are tired and will enjoy the inactivity; make sure the setting is comfortable.

- Choose books that you also enjoy, perhaps one you read as a child; preview the book before presenting it to the children in case there are passages you want to shorten.

- The first time you read a book, state the title and author. Research for interesting facts about the author to share with the children. If there is an illustrator, include that information as well.

- If you are reading to a large group, position yourself so that you are slightly higher than the children so that your voice will project more easily.

- If you are reading to a small group, sit among children in a more intimate placement, which will draw them to you and the book.

- Occasionally stop and ask, "What do you think is going to happen next?"

- Read at a pace that allows children to build mental images of the characters or setting; change your pace to match the action of the story: slow your pace and lower your voice during a suspenseful spot and then speed up when the action does.

- Allow time for discussion based on the children's interest and enthusiasm. Let them voice fears, ask questions, or share their thoughts about the book. Do not turn the discussion into a quiz or need to interpret the story.

- Practice reading aloud, trying to vary your expression or tone of voice.

- Create a display of images or information pertaining to the book you are reading. A map will allow children to pinpoint places mentioned in the story. Pictures, charts, or time lines will also add to the display. Objects or foods mentioned in the book add another dimension.

- Find a stopping place each day that will create suspense, so that the children are eager to get back to the book the next day.

- When you pick up the book the next day, ask children if they remember what had happened just before you stopped reading.

WHAT NOT TO DO

- Don't read a book you do not enjoy; your feelings will be sensed by the children.

- Don't read a book when it becomes obvious that it was a poor choice; previewing the book before presenting it to the children can minimize these kinds of mistakes.

- Don't choose a book with which some of the children are already familiar; they may have heard it at home or seen a version on television or at the movies.

- Don't start a book unless you have enough time to read more than a few pages.

- Don't be fooled by awards. Just because a book has received a national book award does not mean that it is suitable for your particular group of children.

- Don't impose on the children your own interpretations or reactions to the story. Let them express their own understanding and feelings.

HOW TO SELECT BOOKS FOR CHILDREN

Ask yourself the following questions as you select books for the children in your care:

- Is this book sturdy enough to be handled by a group of young children for an extended period of time? (Choose board books, cloth books, and so on for infants and toddlers.)

- Does this book have high-quality, eye-catching artwork that will reflect and/or enrich a child's visual world?

- Does this book invite interaction either by flaps to lift, moving parts, and so on or by invitations to verbal interactions between the adult reader and the children listening?

- Is this book relevant and interesting for children at this age and stage?

- Does this book use characteristics such as alliteration, repetition, rhythm, and/or rhyming text (known to foster early literacy skills) to make it fun to read aloud?

- Does this book tell a good story that can be dramatized with characters' voices and elements of suspense or excitement to hold children's attention?

- Does this book present a sensitive, appreciative portrayal of varied places, cultures, heritages, and abilities?

- Does this book expand children's vocabulary and use of language patterns?

- Does this book encourage exploration and discovery of our natural world?

- Does this book expand children's knowledge of mathematics, science, art, music, geography, history, and so on in a lively, developmentally appropriate manner?

- Does this book demonstrate and promote problem solving?

- Does this book demonstrate and promote character development?

- Is this a book the children will want to listen to and learn to read again and again?

- Am I personally enthusiastic about this book?

- Could I tell a child's parent or a community member what I believe is valuable about this book if they challenged me?

Of course, not every book will meet all the criteria, but focusing on several of these criteria at a time will help you select books that enrich children's listening and learning experiences. These criteria were used to select the following books, which you can add to the list of classic children's books that you already know and love.

Buzzy's Birthday by Harriet Ziefert; illustrated by Emily Bolam

Blue Apple Books, 2004, 24 pages

Ages: infants–4 years

Children can lift the flaps to follow Buzzy as he help his parents prepare for his birthday; an engaging lesson in patience.

I Love You Through and Through by Bernadette Rosseti Shustak; illustrated by Caroline Jay Church

Cartwheel, 2005, 24 pages

Ages: infants–4 years

This book affirms unconditional love as a little boy and his teddy bear act out each message, for example, "I love your topside. I love your bottomside."

Big, Little by Leslie Patricelli

Candlewick Board Edition, 2003, 24 pages

Ages: infants–5 years

A happy baby has fun exploring witty comparisons of big things and little things.

One Moose, Twenty Mice by Clare Beaton

Barefoot Books, 2000, 32 pages

Ages: infants–5 years

This is an animal counting book, which intrigues the children as they look for the partially hidden cat on each page. This book is also available in Spanish, *Un Alce, Veinte Ratones.*

Olivia's Opposites by Ian Falconer

Simon and Schuster, 2002, 12 pages

Ages: 1–4 years

This board book introduces opposites through the humorous poses of Olivia, the pig with personality.

Belly Button Book! by Sandra Boynton

Workman Publishing Co., 2005, 24 pages

Ages: 2–6 years

Bare-bellied hippos on the beach sing to their belly buttons in this board book.

Don't Let the Pigeon Drive the Bus! by Mo Willems

Hyperion, 2003, 36 pages

Ages: 2–7 years

Children will enjoy responding to pigeon's increasingly desperate attempts to take over the bus when the driver takes a break. They will particularly relate to his spectacular temper tantrum.

All by Myself by Aliki

HarperCollins, 2000, 32 pages

Ages: 3–6 years

Rhyming celebration of things children can do all by themselves.

Bear Snores On by Karma Wilson; illustrated by Jane Chapman

Margaret K. McElderry, 2002, 40 pages

Ages: 3–7 years

Introduces hibernation as bear sleeps through a party in his cave, and then wakes to discover what he has missed. The repetitive text encourages participation, and font changes express emotion.

Quack! by Arthur Yorinks; illustrated by Adrienne Yorinks

Harry N. Abrams Inc., 2003, 24 pages

Ages: 3–8 years

Written in the "international language of ducks," this book tells the story of duck's trip to the moon and reflects on the value of friendship; fun to read aloud and together.

Rap a Tap Tap: Here's Bojangles: Think of That by Diane and Leo Dillon

Blue Sky Press, 2002, 32 pages

Ages: 3–8 years

This is a tribute to legendary tap dancer Bill "Bojangles" Robinson with dynamic illustrations, repetition, and rhyme.

Mouse Practice by Emily Arnold McCully

Arthur A. Levine Books, 1999, 32 pages

Ages: 3–8 years

Monk wants to play baseball. He has a musical but unathletic family. He must rely on his own persistence and creativity, reinforced by music, to gain a place on the "big kid's team."

The Kissing Hand by Audrey Penn; illustrated by Ruth Harper and Nancy Leak

Child and Family Press (Child Welfare League of America), 1993, 32 pages

Ages: 3–8 years and parents

This valuable book for early childhood programs describes the simple, powerful ritual that helps a raccoon child feel secure in his mother's love while at school. Share this book with parents.

Eight Animals Bake a Cake by Susan Middleton Elya; illustrated by Lee Chapman

Grosset and Dunlap, 2002, 32 pages

Ages: 4–8 years

Each animal brings an ingredient for the group's cake. Rebus pictures and Spanish words are smoothly embedded in the story. Spanish words are translated in the page borders.

How Are You Peeling? Foods with Moods by Joost Elffers; illustrated by Saxton Freymann

Arthur A. Levine Books, 1999, 48 pages

Ages: 4–8 years and beyond

Uses photographs of funny fruit and vegetable faces to explore moods and feelings; a great starter for making your own food characters.

Mrs. Rose's Garden by Elaine Greenstein

Simon and Schuster, 1996, 32 pages

Ages: 4–8 years

Mrs. Rose is a prize-winning gardener who finds that sharing is even more satisfying than winning.

Houses and Homes by Ann Morris; illustrated by Ken Heyman

HarperTrophy, 1995 (First Edition, HarperCollins, 1992), 32 pages

Ages: 4–8 years

This is a fascinating photographic exploration of homes around the world that takes children beyond their everyday experience. It includes an index and maps with details of each location.

Trashy Town by Andrea Zimmerman and David Clemesha; illustrated by Dan Yaccarino

HarperCollins, 1999, 32 pages

Ages: 4–8 years

Mr. Gilly picks up trash all over town as children cheer him on with an enthusiastic repeating refrain.

Miss Spider's Sunny Patch Kids by David Kirk

Scholastic, 2004, 40 pages

Ages: 4–8 years

The adventurous rhyming tale of how Miss Spider's family grew and grew and everyone was made welcome.

I Like Myself by Karen Beaumont; illustrated by David Catrow

Harcourt Children's Books, 2004, 32 pages

Ages: 4–8 years

A little girl celebrates herself—"stinky toes" and all—with humor and rhyming affirmations that can help any child to feel stronger in a critical world.

Scout: It's Not Easy Raising a Dog by Caroline Heens

Orchard, 2002 (unpaginated)

Ages: 4–8 years

This interactive book uses humor to share tips about dog care; a different approach to nonfiction reading that may work well for children who cannot yet follow a traditional informational text.

The Yawn Heard Round the World by Scott Thomas; illustrated by Tatjana Mai-Wyss

Tricycle Press, 2003, 30 pages

Ages: 4–8 years

Sara protests that she's not sleepy, but her yawn travels around the world and affects everyone from her father to a whale; an imaginative rhyming tale that connects the global family.

Hairs: Pelitos by Sandra Cisneros; illustrated by Terry Ybañez

Dragonfly Books, 1997, 32 pages

Ages: 4–8 years

This bilingual book describes and celebrates the differences among family members' hair.

Bootsie Barker Bites by Barbara Bottner; illustrated by Peggy Rathmann

Putnam Publishing Group, 1992 (Paperstar Books, Reprint Edition, 1997), 32 pages

Ages: 4–8 years

Bootsie Barker bullies. Find out how her petite hostess solves this problem.

Hooway for Wodney Wat by Helen Lester; illustrated by Lynn M. Munsinger

Houghton Mifflin Co., 2002, 32 pages

Ages: 4–8 years

Rodney Rat pronounces "R" as "W," so the other rodents tease him. However, Rodney saves everyone from the class bully; a lesson in alliteration and valuing everyone's contribution.

When Pigasso Met Mootisse by Nina Laden

Chronicle Books, 1998, 40 pages

Ages: 4–10 years

With illustrations and a text that plays on the real art and lives of Picasso and Matisse, this book follows their animal namesakes as they are neighbors, rivals, and, ultimately, friends.

Minnie's Diner by Dayle Ann Dodd; illustrated by John Manders

Candlewick Press, 2004, 40 pages

Ages: 5–8 years

This rhyming tale plays with multiplication as the McFay boys and their formidable father neglect their farm chores to enjoy Minnie's good cooking, each one doubling the previous order.

Dear World by Takaya Noda

Dial Books, 2003, 32 pages

Ages: 5 and up

This book connects children to poetry and to their home on planet Earth as they share a child's notes to the Earth and its creatures.

Duck for President by Doreen Cronin; illustrated by Betsy Lewin

Simon and Schuster, 2004, 40 pages

Ages: 5 and up

Hardworking Duck rises from humble farm animal to the presidency and retires to write his autobiography, providing insights into the political process and many laughs along the way.

Crickwing by Janell Cannon

Harcourt Inc., 2000, 48 pages

Ages: 6 and up

Crickwing the cockroach works with his old enemies, the leaf-cutter ants, to use art to overcome the powerful army ants. Wonderful illustrations and insect notes add to the book's value.

DEVELOPMENTALLY APPROPRIATE PRACTICE

The National Association for the Education of Young Children's (NAEYC's) first position statement on Developmentally Appropriate Practice (DAP) had two main motivations:

- The process of accrediting centers required widely accepted and specific definitions of what constituted excellent practices in early childhood education.

- A proliferation of programs had inappropriate practices and expectations for their children, largely based on premature academic learning.

The original position statement did enhance the early childhood profession, although it was not received with universal acceptance, so a revised position statement clarified some of the previous misunderstandings and expanded the vision of good practices.

Teachers and administrators should keep the principles firmly in mind when making professional decisions and use the statement in conversations with others regarding appropriate practices. Colleagues, administrators, and family members all have their individual understandings of what to do with young children. It is, therefore, useful for every teacher to have a copy of the position statement. In discussion, you can use the position statement to replace the idea of personal opinions with the weight of the professional body of knowledge. The complete statement, *Developmentally Appropriate Practice in Early Childhood Programs,* Revised Edition (1997, NAEYC), can be found at http://www.naeyc.org. Under Information About, click NAEYC, Position Statements, Developmentally Appropriate Practice.

Ethical conduct on the part of personnel in early childhood programs is a fundamental part of developmentally appropriate practice. The first step toward developmentally appropriate practice is to base programs on sound knowledge of child development and to uphold the right of all children to be free from harm. Ethical conduct toward the children's families, our colleagues, and the communities we serve also provides a vital foundation for appropriate early childhood programs. Individual children experience varied circumstances, and each child needs to be treated fairly, respectfully, and with full dignity regardless of those circumstances. The NAEYC Code of Ethical Conduct and Statement of Commitment (Revised April, 2005) upholds the following principle as having priority over all others:

> P-1.1—Above all, we shall not harm children. We shall not participate in practices that are emotionally damaging, physically harmful, disrespectful, degrading, dangerous, exploitative, or intimidating to children.

This principle has precedence over all others in the Code and is the basis for developmentally appropriate practice. The full text of the NAEYC Code of Ethical Conduct and Statement of Commitment, (Revised April, 2005) is available at: http://www.naeyc.org/about/positions/PSETH05.asp.

Another important step toward developmentally appropriate practice is to ensure that early childhood programs meet basic standards of health, safety, and overall quality through the process of licensing by the states in which the programs are located. Regulation and inspection are essential components of guaranteeing freedom from harm for children in child care centers and other early childhood programs. The NAEYC position statement on Licensing and Public Regulation of Early Childhood Programs provides a valuable discussion of the benefits of licensing as well as some important reservations about the current licensing system. You can read the full statement at http://www.naeyc.org/about/positions/pslicense.asp.

The process of accreditation takes an early childhood program beyond the basics to provide care and education for young children that meets carefully developed standards of appropriateness for children from birth to eight years old. When the administrator and staff make a commitment to become an accredited program, they are making a decision to work together to ensure that their environment, curriculum, program-management practices, and interactions with the children, families, and each other all meet the benchmark of developmentally appropriate practice. They will have to invest time in self-examination and open themselves up to feedback from clients as well as scrutiny from external validators.

Complete information about NAEYC accreditation is available at: http://www.naeyc.org; information about the National Early Childhood Program Accreditation is available at http://www. necpa.net; and information about the National Accreditation Commission for Early Care and Education Programs is available at http://www.naccp.org.

GUIDELINES FOR DEVELOPMENTALLY APPROPRIATE PRACTICE

NAEYC's DAP guidelines can be implemented in your daily work with children as described previously and as explained at the NAEYC site.

- Create a Caring Environment among Children and Adults
  You can help children
    - learn personal responsibility.
    - develop constructive relationships with others.
    - respect individual and cultural differences.

  Adults can
    - get to know each child, taking into account individual differences and developmental level.
    - adjust the pace and content of the curriculum so that children can be successful most of the time.
    - bring each child's culture and language into the setting.
    - expect children to be tolerant of others' differences.

- The Curriculum and Schedule Allow Children to Select and Initiate Their Own Activities
  Children can
    - learn through active involvement in a variety of learning experiences.
    - build independence by taking on increasing responsibilities.
    - initiate their own activities to follow their interests.

  Adults can
    - provide a variety of materials and activities that are concrete and real.

- provide a variety of work places and spaces.
- arrange the environment so that children can work alone or in groups.
- extend children's learning by posing problems and asking thought-provoking questions.
- add complexity to tasks as needed.
- model, demonstrate, and provide information so children can progress in their learning.

■ **The Program Is Organized and Integrated So That Children Develop a Deeper Understanding of Key Concepts and Skills**

Children can

- engage in activities that reflect their current interests.
- plan and predict outcomes of their research.
- share information and knowledge with others.

Adults can

- plan related activities and experiences that broaden children's knowledge and skills.
- design curriculum to foster important skills such as literacy and numeracy.
- adapt instruction for children who are ahead or behind age-appropriate expectations.
- plan curriculum so that children achieve important developmental goals.

■ **Activities and Experiences Help Children Develop a Positive Self-Image within a Democratic Community**

Children can

- learn through reading books about other cultures.
- read about current events and discuss how these relate to different cultures.
- accept differences among their peers, including children with disabilities.

Adults can

- provide culturally and nonsexist activities and materials that foster children's self-identity.
- design the learning environment so children can learn new skills while using their native language.
- allow children to demonstrate their learning using their own language.

- Activities and Experiences Develop Children's Awareness of the Importance of Community Involvement
Children
    - are ready and eager to learn about the world outside their immediate environment.
    - are open to considering different ways of thinking or doing things.
    - can benefit from contact with others outside their homes or child care setting.
Adults
    - encourage awareness of the community at large.
    - plan experiences in facilities within the community.
    - bring outside resources and volunteers into the child care setting.
    - encourage children to plan their involvement based on their own interests.

Professional Associations for Early Childhood Educators and Administrators

National Association for the Education of Young Children (NAEYC)
1509 16th Street, NW
Washington, DC 20036
800-424-2460
http://www.naeyc.org
E-mail: membership@naeyc.org

Specific membership benefits:

Comprehensive members receive all the benefits of regular membership plus annually receive five or six books immediately after their release by NAEYC.

Regular and student member benefits:

- Six issues of *Young Children,* which includes timely articles on pertinent issues, as well as suggestions and strategies for enhancing children's learning

- Reduced registration fees at NAEYC-sponsored local and national conferences and seminars

- Discounted prices on hundreds of books, videos, brochures, and posters from NAEYC's extensive catalog of materials

- Access to the Members Only Web site, including links to additional resources and chat sites for communication with other professionals

National Association of Child Care Professionals (NACCP)
P.O. Box 90723
Austin, TX 78709
800-537-1118
http://www.naccp.org

Specific membership benefits:

Management Tools of the Trade™

Your membership provides complete and free access (a $79 value) to these effective management tools that provide technical assistance in human resource management. In addition, you will receive NACCP's quarterly trade journals, *Professional Connections©, Teamwork©,* and *Caring for Your Children©,* to help you stay on top of hot issues in child care. Each edition also includes a Tool of the Trade™.

National Child Care Association (NCCA)
1016 Rosser St.
Conyers, GA 30012
800-543-7161
http://www.nccanet.org

Specific membership benefits:

As the only recognized voice in Washington, DC, NCCA has great influence on our legislators. Professional development opportunities are also available.

Association for Education International (ACEI)
The Olney Professional Building
17904 Georgia Avenue, Suite 215
Olney, MD 20832
800-423-2563 or 301-570-2122
301-570-2212 (fax)
http://www.acei.org

ACEI is an international organization dedicated to promoting the best educational practices throughout the world.

Specific membership benefits:

- Workshops and travel/study tours abroad

- Four issues per year of the *Childhood Education* journal and the *Journal of Research in Childhood Education*

- Hundreds of resources for parents and teachers, including books, pamphlets, audiotapes, and videotapes

National AfterSchool Association (NAA)
1137 Washington Street
Boston, MA 02124
617-298-5012
617-298-5022 (fax)
http://www.naaweb.org

NAA is a national organization dedicated to providing information, technical assistance, and resources concerning children in out-of-school programs. Members include teachers, policy makers, and administrators representing all public, private, and community-based sectors of after-school programs.

Specific membership benefits:

- A subscription to the NAA journal, *School-Age Review*

- A companion membership in state affiliates

- Discounts on NAA publications and products

- Discount on NAA annual conference registration

- Opportunity to be an NAA accreditation endorser

- Public policy representatives in Washington, DC

OTHER ORGANIZATIONS TO CONTACT

The Children's Defense Fund
25 E. St. NW
Washington, DC 20001
202-628-8787
http://www.childrensdefense.org

National Association for Family Child Care
P.O. Box 10373
Des Moines, IA 50306
800-359-3817
http://www.nafcc.org
Journal: *The National Perspective*

National Black Child Development Institute
1023 15th Ave. NW
Washington, DC 20002
202-833-2220
http://www.nbcdi.org

National Head Start Association
1651 Prince Street
Alexandria, VA 22314
703-739-0875
http://www.nhsa.org
Journal: *Children and Families*

International Society for the Prevention of Child Abuse and Neglect
25 W. 560 Geneva Road, Suite L2C
Carol Stream, IL 60188
630-221-1311
http://ispcan.org
Journal: *Child Abuse and Neglect: The International Journal*

Council for Exceptional Children
1110N. Glebe Road, Suite 300
Arlington, VA 22201
888-CEC-SPED
http://www.cec.sped.org
Journal: *CEC Today*

National Association for Bilingual Education
Union Center Plaza
810 First Street, NE
Washington, DC 20002
http://www.nabe.org
Journal: *NABE Journal of Research and Practice*

International Reading Association
800 Barksdale Road
P.O. Box 8139
Newark, DE 19714
800-336-READ
http://www.reading.org
Journal: *The Reading Teacher*

National Education Organization (NEA)
1201 16th St. NW
Washington, DC 20036
202-833-4000
http://www.nea.org
Journals: *Works4Me* and *NEA Focus,* by online subscription

Zero to Three: National Center for Infants, Toddlers, and Families
2000M Street NW, Suite 200
Washington, DC 20036
202-638-1144
http://www.zerotothree.org
Journal: *Zero to Three*

RESOURCES

BOOKS

Child Guidance, Discipline, and Classroom Community

Albert, Linda, Ph.D. (2003). *Cooperative Discipline: Teacher's Handbook*. Circle Pines, MN: AGS Publishing.

Bailey, Becky A., Ph.D. (2000, Rev. 2001). *Conscious Discipline: 7 Basic Skills for Brain Smart Classroom Management*. Oviedo, FL: Loving Guidance.

Faber, Adele, & Mazlish, Elaine. (1980, Afterword © 1999). *How to Talk So Kids Will Listen and Listen So Kids Will Talk*. New York: Avon Books.

Hewitt, Deborah. (1997). *So This Is Normal, Too? Teachers and Parents Working Out Developmental Issues in Young Children*. St. Paul, MN: Redleaf Press.

Kinnell, Gretchen. (2002). *No Biting: Policy and Practice for Toddler Programs*. St. Paul, MN: Redleaf Press.

Marion, Marian. (1991 edition). *Guidance of Young Children*. New York: Macmillan Publishing Company.

Reynolds, Eleanor. (1990). *Guiding Young Children: A Child-Centered Approach*. Mountain View, CA: Mayfield Publishing Company.

Whelan, Mary Steiner. (2000). *But They Spit, Scratch, and Swear! The Do's and Don'ts of Behavior Guidance with School-Age Children*. Minneapolis: A-ha! Communications.

Staff Management, Support, and Leadership

Baker, Amy, & Manfredi/Petitt, Lynn. (2004). *Relationships, the Heart of Quality Care: Creating Community among Adults in Child Care Settings.* St. Paul, MN: Redleaf Press.

Bloom, Paula J. (1997). *A Great Place to Work: Improving Conditions for Staff in Young Children's Programs* (Rev. ed.). Washington, DC: National Association for the Education of Young Children.

Bloom, Paula J. (2000). *Circle of Influence: Implementing Shared Decision Making and Participative Management.* Lake Forest, IL: New Horizons.

Carter, Margie, & Curtis, Deb. (1998). *The Visionary Director: A Handbook for Dreaming, Organizing and Improvising in Your Center.* St. Paul, MN: Redleaf Press.

Moravcik, Eva, Freeman, Nancy, & Feeney, Stephanie. (2000). *Teaching the NAEYC Code of Ethical Conduct.* Washington, DC: National Association for the Education of Young Children.

Reynolds, Arthur, Wang, Margaret, & Walberg, Herbert. (2003). *Early Childhood Programs for a New Century.* Chicago: Child Welfare League of America.

Sciarra, Dorothy June, & Dorsey, Anne. (2001). *Leaders and Supervisors in Child Care Programs.* Clifton Park, NY: Thomson Delmar Learning.

Talan, Teri, & Bloom, Paula J. (2004). *Program Administration Scale: Measuring Early Childhood Leadership and Management.* New York: Teachers College Press.

Whitebook, Marcy, & Bellm, Dan. (1998). *Taking on Turnover: An Action Guide for Child Care Center Teachers and Directors.* Washington, DC: National Center for the Early Childhood Workforce.

Business and Program Management

Biasetto, Wendy. (1995). *The Ultimate Guide to Forms for Early Childhood Programs.* Sarasota, FL: Learning Expo.

Hearron, Patricia F., & Hildebrand, Verna F. (2002). *Management of Child Development Centers* (5th ed.). Upper Saddle River, NJ: Prentice Hall.

Jack, Gail. (2005). *The Business of Child Care: Management and Financial Strategies.* Clifton Park, NY: Thomson Delmar Learning.

Morgan, Gwen G. (1999). *The Bottom Line for Children's Programs: What You Need to Know to Manage the Money.* Watertown, MA: Steam Press

Schiller, Pam, & Carter Dyke, Patricia. (2001). *The Practical Guide to Quality Child Care.* Beltsville, MD: Gryphon House.

Curriculum, Development, and Approaches to Learning

Bredekamp, Sue, & Copple, Carol. (1997). *Developmentally Appropriate Practice in Early Childhood Programs* (Rev. ed.). Washington, DC: National Association for the Education of Young Children.

Derman-Sparks, Louise, & the A. B. C. Task Force. (1989). *Anti-Bias Curriculum: Tools for Empowering Young Children.* Washington, DC: National Association for the Education of Young Children.

Dombro, Amy Laura, Colker, Laura J., & Trister Dodge, Diane. (1999). *The Creative Curriculum for Infants and Toddlers* (Rev. ed.). Washington, DC: Teaching Strategies.

Gardner, Howard. (2000). *Intelligence Reframed: Multiple Intelligences for the 21st Century.* New York: Basic Books.

Jones, Elizabeth, & Nimmo, John. (1994). *Emergent Curriculum.* Washington, DC: National Association for the Education of Young Children.

Phillips, Deborah A., & Shonkoff, Jack P. (eds.). (2000). *From Neurons to Neighborhoods: The Science of Early Childhood Development.* Washington, DC: National Academies Press.

Rockwell, Robert. (2003). *Partnering with Parents: 29 Easy Programs to Involve Parents in the Early Learning Process.* Beltsville, MD: Gryphon House.

Trister Dodge, Diane, Colker, Laura J., Heroman, Cate, & Bickart, Toni S. (2002). *The Creative Curriculum for Preschool* (4th ed.). Clifton Park, NY: Thomson Delmar Learning.

Winsler, Adam, & Berk, Laura. (1995). *Scaffolding Children's Learning: Vygotsky and Early Childhood Education.* Washington, DC: National Association for the Education of Young Children.

Wolfgang, Charles H., & Wolfgang, Mary E. (1992). *School for Young Children: Developmentally Appropriate Practices.* Needham Heights, MA: Allyn and Bacon.

Wurm, Julianne P. (2005). *Working in the Reggio Way: A Beginner's Guide for American Teachers.* St. Paul, MN: Redleaf Press.

Assessment and Evaluation of Children and Programs

Harms, Thelma, Clifford, Richard M., & Cryer, Debby. (2005) *Early Childhood Environment Rating Scale* (Rev. ed.). New York: Teachers College Press.

Harms, Thelma, Clifford, Richard M., & Cryer, Debby. (2003). *Infant/Toddler Environment Rating Scale* (Rev. ed.). New York: Teachers College Press.

MacDonald, Sharon. (1997). *The Portfolio and Its Use: A Road Map for Assessment.* Little Rock, AR: Southern Early Childhood Association.

INTERNET RESOURCES

Child Guidance, Discipline, and Classroom Community
http://www.beckybailey.com/
Dr. Becky Bailey's site provides immediately usable discipline tips and activities as well as research-based resources to create your school family.

http://www.rch.org.au/ecconnections/
This Australian Web site has a wonderful compendium of international early childhood links and great fact sheets for parents and providers on topics such as biting, sharing, and temper tantrums.

Business and Program Management
http://www.acf.hhs.gov
The Child Care Bureau site gives directors important information on federal programs related to child care and links to state and local resources.

http://www.ccw.org/
The Center for the Child Care Workforce provides links to wage incentive programs in your state and a wealth of information for understanding and strengthening child care funding and wages.

http://www.childcareexchange.com/
When center directors first discover the *Child Care Information Exchange* magazine, they ask, "Why didn't someone tell me sooner?" This is the dynamic, comprehensive Exchange Web site.

http://www.childproviderlaw.com/
Ronald V. McGuckin is a frequent presenter at early childhood conferences. His Web site has a generous helping of valuable legal information for child care administrators.

http://www.clasp.org/
The Center for Law and Social Policy provides access to up-to-date information on policies that impact low-income families. This information is helpful for grant writing and advocacy.

http://www.cwla.org
The Child Welfare League of America's information on Child Care and Development is helpful when writing grants and business proposals and when advocating for early childhood programs.

http://www.earlychildhoodfocus.org/
This site provides up-to-the-minute news on current topics in early childhood care and education.

http://www.ehsnrc.org
Not just for Early Head Start administrators and teachers, this site has a good collection of full-text documents on management and early teaching topics.

http://www.firstclassteachers.org/
The American Federation of Teachers site for early childhood educators brings teachers together in support of high quality for children and worthy compensation for staff; great stories are included!

http://www.freetranslation.com/
This is an invaluable site for today's diverse communities. You can enter a brief text and receive a free translation from English to French, Spanish, Chinese, and so on, which is great for newsletter items and the like.

http://www.icebreakers.us/
This site gives a terrific list of ice breakers that could be used for meetings, parent/professional workshops, and so on. Many could be adapted. Select with sensitivity for your group.

http://www.kindercare.org/
This is the state of the art for Web marketing of child care, including virtual tours and information on accreditation. It shows new directors current topics of importance to parents.

http://nieer.org/about/
The National Institute for Early Education Research at Rutgers University seeks to support early childhood initiatives by providing objective, nonpartisan information based on research.

http://www.resourcesforchildcare.org/
Although this Web site is primarily for providers in Minnesota, it contains a good introduction to the business side of child care and a practical discussion of business relationships with parents.

http://www.wested.org/
This site links educators and administrators to in-depth research and policy trends that are valuable for grant writing, advocacy, and long-term strategic planning.

Curriculum, Development, and Approaches to Learning
http://123child.com/
This site has many ideas for preschool learning activities as well as articles written in a straightforward style on everything from grant writing to Tourette's syndrome.

http://www.ascd.org/
The Association for Supervision and Curriculum Development is primarily for K–12, but its site contains excellent information and resources on topics relevant to all educational settings.

http://www.bankstreet.edu/
The Bank Street College of Education provides a user-friendly guide to help train volunteers and providers who have not had formal education in supporting early literacy skills. It also gives directors a peek into a long established program that emphasizes hands-on learning in a warm, communal setting.

http://www.cccrt.org/
Here are the resources of the Creative Pre-School in Tallahassee, Florida, a thoroughly researched model program where children learn as they play and interact with peers and skilled staff.

http://www.educationworld.com
This Web site searches education Web sites only for useful articles, lesson plans, and so on.

http://www.highscope.org/
This is a great site for research and resources to support hands-on programs that encourage children's initiative, decision-making, and responsibility.

http://www.kiddyhouse.com/
This Web site includes intriguing interactive online activities for school-agers such as All about Frogs and Build-A-Prairie. It also provides related stories, songs, and classroom activities.

http://latelier.org/
Colorful, beautiful, hopeful, and informative, this site provides insight into the Reggio Emilia approach to early childhood education.

http://lessonplanz.com/
Unlike many lesson plan sites, this site links educators to multiple free ideas that are hands-on and open-ended.

http://www.literacyconnections.com/
This site is a goldmine for any teacher or administrator interested in knowing more about nurturing lifelong literacy, including links to free downloadable books.

http://www.teachingstrategies.com/
The Web site for the Creative Curriculum includes articles on a variety of topics that are helpful to child care administrators and teachers; some are only accessible to members.

http://www.turnthepage.com/
Bev Bos's Web site is rich with books and music, products she has developed, and articles that reflect her bold philosophy of open-ended exploration with adults as "consultants."

Health
http://www.aap.org/
Everything you and your families wanted to know about children's health according to the American Academy of Pediatrics; an extremely informative and up-to-date site.

http://www.brightfutures.org/
The site for the Georgetown University national health promotion initiative includes materials for families and even an online activity book for children to encourage healthy choices.

http://www.cdc.gov
From "airbags" to "zoonotic diseases" (diseases spread from animals to people), this Centers for Disease Control Web site provides a wide variety of health topics affecting children.

http://www.henrythehand.com/
Dr. William P. Sawyer promotes the essential practice of hand washing and hand awareness through an appealing character called Henry the Hand; this site is loaded with resources and a cute song.

http://www.insurekidsnow.gov/
This site links directors to the resources available in their state for providing health insurance for all the children in their care.

http://www.kidshealth.org/
This Nemours Foundation site is rich with information and connections and has a great section for children with topics that range from understanding genes to help coping with family fights.

Family Involvement
http://www.iamyourchild.org/
This is a very helpful site for teachers and administrators who want to support and empower parents; this site is full of tips, stories, and connections that parents can use.

http://www.tnpc.com/
The National Parenting Center has a wealth of articles, by experts such as Dr. Penelope Leach, which teachers and administrators can share with parents.

Special Needs
http://www.nectac.org/
The National Early Childhood Technical Assistance Center provides comprehensive information and resources for including children with special needs in early childhood programs.

http://www.nichcy.org/
This site is loaded with information and resources for inclusion of children and youth with disabilities, including "Zigawhat!" pages for school-age children with special needs.

Computer Programs for Children
These programs can easily be found online by searching the Web sites of major retailers or Amazon.com.

I Spy School Days
Children develop skills in visual discrimination, creative writing, math concepts, and more as they enjoy classification games, hidden item games, puzzles, and riddles.

Learn to Play Chess with Fritz and Chesster
Children learn chess basics through arcade games as they help Fritz defeat King Black.

Mozart's Magic Flute: The Music Game
Children learn to identify musical instruments and music patterns.

Pajama Sam 2: Thunder and Lightning Aren't So Frightening
Children use problem solving skills to help Sam fix the weather machines at Wide World Weather headquarters.

Pajama Sam 3: You Are What You Eat From Your Head to Your Feet

Children learn about the food pyramid as they help Sam bring peace between the "junk foods" and the nutritious foods.

Putt-Putt Enters the Race

Children use sequencing and memory skills as they prepare Putt-Putt for the Cartown 500 and incidentally learn about safety skills such as dialing 911 and wearing safety helmets.

Spy Fox: Operation Ozone

Children must use logic and concentration to help Spy Fox save the ozone layer and the world from Poodles Galore's giant hairspray space station.

Zoombinis Logical Journey

Children solve math puzzles involving the Zoombinis features as variables as they help the Zoombinis with their quest for freedom and a new homeland.

VIDEOS/DVDs FOR CAREGIVERS

Child Care and Children with Special Needs

(34 minutes)

This two-video set provides training on the meaning of the Americans with Disabilities Act for child care programs and appropriate ways to provide care for children with disabilities.

National Association for the Education of Young Children

http://www.naeyc.org/

Daily Dilemmas: Coping with Challenges

(28 minutes)

This video offers techniques to help with transitions and challenging behaviors.

National Association for the Education of Young Children
http://www.naeyc.org/

Diversity and Conflict Management

(27 minutes)

Part of the "Diversity" video series, this video introduces the RERUN conflict management process through realistic role-plays of parent–provider communication.

Magna Systems

http://www.magnasystemsvideos.com/

Developing Children's Eating Habits

(18 minutes)

This video describes how caregivers influence preschool children's food habits and suggests developmentally appropriate practices.

Colorado State University

971-491-7334

Domestic Violence and Childhood Trauma

(29 minutes)

This video provides insight into the deep and long-lasting effects that domestic violence can have on children in the home where the violence is taking place. It also gives an approach to healing.

Magna Systems

http://www.magnasystemsvideos.com/

Essential Connections: Ten Keys to Culturally Sensitive Child Care

(36 minutes)

This video illustrates effective principles to promote culturally sensitive child care environments such as "Work toward Representative Staffing."

California Department of Education

http://www.cde.ca.gov/re/pn/rc/

Men Caring for Young Children

(30 minutes)

This video explores men working with infants to school-agers in a variety of educational environments.

National Association for the Education of Young Children

http://www.naeyc.org/

Parents: Our Most Important Resource

(27 minutes)

This video places a strong emphasis on respectful communication with parents throughout the process of screening and assessment for their child.

Magna Systems

http://www.magnasystemsvideos.com/

Promoting Language and Literacy

(29 minutes)

Caregivers and parents work together to provide relationships and skilled interactions to support infant/toddler language and literacy development.

Magna Systems

http://www.magnasystemsvideos.com/

Seeds of Change—Leadership and Staff Development

(30 minutes)

This video explores options for staff empowerment and professional development. Principal Joseph Copeland is an excellent role model for proactive leadership.

National Association for the Education of Young Children

http://www.naeyc.org/

Set Straight on Bullies

(18 minutes)

This "docudrama" is designed to prompt discussion and planning to prevent bullying.

National School Safety Center

http://www.nssc1.org/videos/

Shaping Youngest Minds

(24 minutes)

This video explores the role of attachment and experience in brain development.

Learning Seed Educational Videos and CD-ROMs

http://www.learningseed.com/

Supporting Children in Resolving Conflicts

(30 minutes)

This video explains six problem solving steps that children from toddlers to school-agers can use to resolve conflict through real scenes of successful conflict resolution.

High/Scope Educational Research Foundation

http://www.highscope.org/

The Brain and Early Childhood

(30–35 minutes)

These videos explore both the science of brain development and best practices for early learners.

Association for Supervision and Curriculum Development

http://shop.ascd.org/

The Creative Curriculum Video

(37 minutes)

This video clearly demonstrates how learning centers work for children whether the program has adopted the Creative Curriculum itself or is adapting it for another center-based curriculum.

Teaching Strategies, Inc.

http://www.teachingstrategies.com/

The High/Scope Curriculum: The Daily Routine

(17 minutes)

This video examines each component of the High/Scope daily routine and can be used as a basis for teachers and administrators to reflect on the daily routine in their programs.

High/Scope Educational Research Foundation

http://www.highscope.org/

The Role of Teachers and Parents

(29 minutes)

This video examines the role of teachers and parents in developing early literacy in young children.

Magna Systems

http://www.magnasystemsvideos.com/

Welcoming All Children

(28 minutes)

This is a very positive presentation on how to implement an inclusive early childhood setting.

National Association for the Education of Young Children

http://www.naeyc.org/

CASE STUDIES

THE VALUE OF THE CASE STUDY APPROACH

A case study provides a story and situation that reflects the real-life experiences of children, families, care providers, educators, and administrators. Often, we can relate to that story because it is similar to a situation that we have experienced, are experiencing, or may soon experience. We feel less alone and gain insights as we connect the case study to our own experience. The following case studies have the added value of specific recommendations of actions to pursue and actions to avoid, as well as links to additional resources for each situation.

You may find it valuable to reflect on future situations using the case study format. First, describe the realities of the situation as factually and objectively as possible, considering all the key factors and maintaining a developmental perspective. Then, write out the responses you want to pursue and the responses you want to avoid. In addition, you can identify one or two helpful resources that will empower you to make the most of the opportunity for this particular child.

Case Study 1: "What happened to Melinda?"—Responding to Child Abuse, Neglect, or Abandonment

Melinda is a two-year and three-month-old girl who has been attending Sunshine Child Care for six months. On a typical day, Melinda's mother brings her to the classroom, chats with the teacher and Melinda, follows a simple routine to help Melinda put her things in her cubby, and leaves for work. Melinda then becomes involved in the classroom activities, although she is more of an observer than a participator. Her verbal and motor skills are within the range for her age; however, she speaks very little with other children, usually confining herself to quiet dialogue with her teacher, Joanne. She allows other children to take toys from her and waits for Joanne or another teacher to help. This Monday morning, Melinda's mother drops her off by placing her in Joanne's arms and running out of the classroom door. She does not make eye contact with Joanne, nor speak with her or Melinda. Melinda screams whenever Joanne attempts to put her on the floor to inter-act with the other children and even reaches up and scratches Joanne's face. When another child approaches, Melinda screams louder and leans over to bite the child. Joanne notices that Melinda has a strong smell and that she is wearing the same clothes that she wore to go home on Friday evening. They are stained and damp and her diaper is soaked and has a bowel movement in it. Joanne sits down with Melinda at the snack table and offers her a simple snack, which Melinda devours. Joanne asks her co-teacher to cover the classroom and takes Melinda to center director Rhonda's office. Joanne tells Rhonda that she is very concerned and believes some-thing happened to Melinda over the weekend.

Solutions:

- Know state and federal law regarding child abuse, neglect, and abandonment, including your responsibilities and time frames for reporting.

- Know the indicators for abuse and neglect.

- Take the indicators of abuse and neglect seriously.

- Take teachers' concerns seriously; they are with the child every day.

- Document factual observations, including relevant dates and times, and support teachers in documenting their observations.

- Promptly report serious concerns to the child abuse hotline or law enforcement agency responsible for investigating abuse and neglect in your state.

- Inform your state child care licensing representative or equivalent agency representative that you are responding to a possible case of abuse or neglect related to a child at your center and consult with them as needed.

- Inform your governing board or equivalent supervisory body in accordance with program policy.

- Maintain confidentiality at all times regarding the names and specifics of the case when communicating with anyone other than the appropriate investigating agency.

- Continue to provide high-quality comfort and care for the child.

- Create a written policy and procedure in accordance with state and federal law for responding to all incidents of suspected abuse, neglect, and abandonment related to the program, including allegations against program personnel.

Responses to avoid:

- Ignore indicators of abuse and neglect or fail to report abandonment within mandated time frames.

- Investigate the situation yourself by interrogating the child or the family. When individuals investigate and interrogate independently, they impede the ability of law enforcement and social services to provide appropriate protection for the child, support for the family, and prosecution of abusers. They may also increase the trauma to the child by inappropriate questioning.

- Breach confidentiality.

- Focus on blaming, labeling, or shaming. It is particularly important to avoid unprofessional discussion of any situation of inadequate parenting/care in front of the child. No matter how difficult the situation, this is still the child's reality. The child needs stability, reassurance, support, and constructive counsel, not identification as a member of a "bad" family.

Case Study 2: "I don't want him picking them up anymore!"— Handling Custody Disputes

Julio, aged five years and one month, and Elana, aged three years and six months, have been attending Palm Park Child Development Center since they were six weeks old. At closing time on Wednesday evening, the children's mother, Eloisa, asks to speak to center director, Irma. She informs Irma that she has separated from the children's husband and they will be getting a divorce. She tells Irma that she does not want their father to pick the children up anymore nor to get any information about the children nor any of the children's papers. She tells Irma, "From now on, you will only be dealing with me."

Solutions:

- Reflect the feelings and concerns behind the words used by a distressed parent; seek first to understand and to show understanding and only then to be understood.

- Explain the legal requirements and program policy regarding release of children, information, and documentation to both custodial parents.

- Ensure that each parent understands that you are not at liberty to "deny family members access to their child's classroom or program setting unless access is denied by court order or other legal restriction." (NAEYC Code of Ethical Conduct, P–2.1) Ensure that each parent understands that this also means you cannot deny access to the child, or information or documentation pertinent to that child.

- Negotiate an appropriate response to the parent's concern. Such responses could range from offering information on obtaining a court order and links to community resources for a parent experiencing domestic violence, to seeking a formal conference with either or both parents to provide the program's professional support to prepare for the family change and to reduce the inevitable stress on the children.

- State unequivocally that the program's job is to care for the children in accordance with the law.

- Document all informal and formal parent conferences and meetings, including dates and times.

- Recognize the volatility of custodial disputes and be prepared to take appropriate action, including contacting law enforcement when needed.

- Train staff to respond effectively and appropriately to custodial conflict.

- Create a written policy and procedure in accordance with state and federal law for responding to changes in family structure due to divorce and separation, including responding to custodial disputes.

Responses to avoid:

- Breach confidentiality.

- Take sides with one parent over another. The NAEYC Code of Ethical Conduct states, "P-2.14—In cases where family members are in conflict with one another, we shall work openly, sharing our observations of the child, to help all parties involved make informed decisions. We shall refrain from becoming an advocate for one party."

■ Be intimidated by a parent who is angry about a change in his or her life to become involved in that change to the detriment of his or her children, other children in the program, and the program's reputation and ability to operate.

■ Become defensive or hostile to a parent, even when the parent is "coming on strong." Instead seek a quiet comfortable place where you can sit together and discuss similarities and differences in your ideas. Remember that you are the professional.

■ Allow a parent to become abusive or inappropriate with you or any of your staff. Remind parents that they are in a program that serves children and that everyone in the program follows a standard of conduct that can serve as a good model for the children.

Case Study 3: "Will Anton be welcome?"—Including Children with Special Needs

Anton is a two-and-a-half-year-old boy with cerebral palsy. He will be starting First Church Early Learning Center on Monday. When his mother, Hannah, called the center director, Mary, two weeks ago, she first asked Mary if there was a space in the twos classroom. When Mary confirmed that there was, Hannah asked about the center's tuition, accreditation, and hours of operation. Apparently satisfied with Mary's answers, Hannah made an appointment to visit the center. Then she said, "Oh, by the way, my son, Anton, has cerebral palsy and has to use a walking frame, will that be a problem?" Mary assured her that all children were welcome at First Church ELC. Hannah cried and told her that First Church was the 10th center she had called. She stated that she had learned to ask if there was a space and then mention Anton's cerebral palsy. When she identified Anton's condition first, many center directors told her that they had no space, even though the local child care resource and referral agency had assured her that those centers had openings for two-year-olds.

Solutions:

■ Know the Americans with Disabilities Act and the Individuals with Disabilities Education Act and know your responsibilities as a child care provider and an educator under these laws.

- Provide your staff with professional development opportunities to become better equipped to serve children with legally defined special needs.

- Use the Internet, library, support groups, and specialists to learn more about the specific conditions and abilities/disabilities of children enrolled in the program.

- Share this information with staff members.

- Have an enrollment form and procedure that provides for all parents to describe their child's special needs, fears, interests, and the strategies that help that child.

- Include space for any parent to provide detailed information regarding feeding, rest, toileting, continuous medication needs, and other important aspects of care for the child.

- Provide an informative program brochure, a printed fee sheet, a center tour, a written parent handbook, and a personal orientation for all families enrolling their child in the program.

- Provide for a gradual start for families who prefer that their child "phase in" to the program, with clear guidelines agreed upon in advance to structure this process.

- Encourage parent-to-parent communication through parent meetings, special events, a network of buddies for new families, and so on to help all new families make a smooth and positive transition into the program and to help overcome barriers between families, which might impact the children's care.

- Monitor the progress of all children and conduct "walk around management visits" to classrooms with newly enrolled children to see and hear firsthand how the children are developing in their new classroom.

- Provide prompt, encouraging, specific, and constructive support for teachers who are involved in caring for a child with significant special needs.

- Ensure that parents have links to the support groups and resources that will help them provide the best home possible for their child.

- Work with families, specialists, and other members of multidisciplinary teams to provide needed therapies and interventions for the child.

- Remember that high-quality developmentally appropriate practice reduces the significance of special needs and that everyone has "special needs."

Responses to avoid:

- Judge, label, or blame other center directors.

- Ignore the reality that children with significant special needs may require more one-on-one time and more energy than typically developing children or downplay teacher's concerns and legitimate needs.

- Pretend the special need does not exist when responding to other children's questions. Instead, talk simply and factually and remember to ask children for their answer to the question and then provide appropriate information to correct misconceptions.

- Discuss confidential information about a child with special needs or information about their family with any person or agency without a specific written release from the appropriate family member, except when required to do so by child protection laws.

- Charge a higher fee for service for a child with special needs as that is both unethical and against the law under the Americans with Disabilities Act.

For more information on the Americans with Disabilities Act and the Individuals with Disabilities Education Act, go to these Web sites:

http://www.usdoj.gov/crt/ada/adahom1.htm

http://www.usdoj.gov/crt/ada/cguide.htm

Case Study 4: "All she does here is play!"—Promoting Developmentally Appropriate Practice and Play-Based Learning

Tonya, aged 3 years and 11 months, runs into her classroom at Play and Learn Academy every morning and quickly becomes involved in the learning center activities that LaTasha and Jeannette, her teachers, have ready for the children. She has been attending the center for 10 months. The regular "Ages and Stages Questionnaire" screenings that the center conducts on all the children with the parents' written consent show that Tonya is developing very well in all areas. She is very verbal, loves to help around the room, and is equally absorbed whether engaged in dramatic play with friends, painting at the easel, or sorting plastic insects to match pictures in an insect book at the nature table. Center director, Marvin, has noticed Tonya's mother, Esther, studying the artwork displayed in the hallway and talking at length with other mothers in the parking lot. This Friday afternoon, Esther comes early to pick up Tonya and asks to speak with Marvin. She tells him that she is tired of all this play and that it is time for some learning for her daughter. She lets him know that she is not the only parent who thinks that the children are getting too old for just playing and who wants to see more academics in the program. She wants to be sure that her child will not be left behind in school.

Solutions:

- Reflect the feelings and concerns behind the words used by a distressed parent; seek first to understand and to show understanding and only then to be understood.

- Explain the program's philosophy of developmentally appropriate practice and the manner in which academic, school readiness learning opportunities are integrated into the children's play-based experiences.

- Provide reasons for choosing developmentally appropriate practice, remembering that individuals are persuaded by a variety of different means; for example, some are most influenced by research data, while others need opportunities to observe and see for themselves.

- Listen for cultural concerns or signs that a parent has unhappy memories of school and share understanding of these concerns, while providing an alternate vision of a positive future rather than a negative repetition of past injuries.

- Listen for legitimate and accurate criticisms of your program and seek to involve parents in making constructive changes.

- Focus on the wide range of skills needed for success in school and careers today, particularly the higher-order questioning and thinking skills that will be needed as students reach more complex levels in their studies and more complex problems in the workplace.

- Create a written philosophy and select a well-documented curriculum or combination of curricula for the program. Take time at enrollment and orientation and through parent work-shops, newsletters, and other program communications to share the program's philosophy and curriculum with families.

- Involve family members from the start in selecting new materials and curricula, while reserving the right to veto inappropriate practices.

- Document children's learning through use of work samples, audio and video recordings, and written observations.

- Compile these in a portfolio for each child, which can also include the results of checklists, developmental screenings, and other appropriate measures.

- Share these regularly with parents so that they can see for themselves the progress that their child is making and where they may need extra help or attention.

- Provide teachers with time to create well-documented cur-rent displays of children's work that highlight the learning process.

- Be prepared to provide referrals to alternate programs for par-ents who have an unchanging preference for a curriculum that differs significantly from that of your program and reassure them that your program's door remains open in the future.

Responses to avoid:

- Dismiss or belittle parental concerns about curriculum and teaching methodology in your program.

- Ignore legitimate parental concerns with program practices or teacher competence. Always document and follow up on concerns.

- Fail to provide parents with realistic information about pro-gram practices and how these relate to current school readi-ness standards at enrollment and throughout their child's stay in your program.

- Exclude parents from opportunities to learn more about developmentally appropriate practice such as teacher pro-fessional development workshops.

- Exclude parents from opportunities to select curriculum approaches, materials, and assessment tools from among a variety of developmentally appropriate choices.

Case Study 5: "Keeping up with Paul"—Managing Biting and Other Harmful Behaviors

Eighteen-month-old Paul has been an active child ever since he started to attend Mountain View Children's Center. Even in the infant room, he took shorter naps than most of the babies, and he was scooting around the room while his age mates were still sitting on the play rug where the teacher put them. His movements are rapid. His speech seems to be a little behind the other toddlers. It takes all his teachers' energy to keep up with him. Now, he is biting the other children. The teachers are getting very frustrated and have complained to center director, Mae Lin, that he sometimes seems to bite "for no reason at all." The incident reports are mounting up. The parents have deduced that Paul is the biter and many are also coming to Mae Lin to complain. In fact, three of them have threatened to withdraw their children from the program unless she "gets rid" of Paul. This would be a serious loss of tuition. Mae Lin knows that Paul's dad, a single father, really relies on Mountain View as his partner in raising Paul.

Solutions:

- Before children begin biting, provide families with simple, easy-to-read information on why children bite and how to respond effectively. Provide this information again when children begin to exhibit biting behavior.

- Have an easily accessible parent resource area that includes books, articles, and computer access to more in-depth information on biting that parents can check out at their convenience.

- Have a written policy and procedure on the program's response to biting and other hurtful behaviors that is shared with all staff and families at orientation and require documentation of agreement to abide by this and other program policies.

- Include reasons not to disenroll children for age-appropriate biting behavior as well as guidelines for disenrollment when that is in the best interests of all children concerned.

- Provide teachers with training on effective responses to biting behavior such as focusing immediate attention on the "victim" rather than the biter.

- Provide teachers with training on techniques for preventing and responding to other harmful or difficult behaviors.

- Provide adequate teacher–child ratios to ensure safe supervision.

- Frequently monitor classrooms with friendly but alert "walk around management" to ensure that staff members are actively aware of children's behavior and are providing constructive guidance.

- Reflect the feelings and concerns behind the words used by a distressed parent; seek first to understand and to show understanding and only then to be understood.

- When appropriate, remind distressed parents that their child may bite or engage in some hurtful behavior at some point in the future and that they will then want time for their child to learn more acceptable ways to express himself or herself.

- Learn about HIV/AIDS and the transmission of other diseases caused by bloodborne pathogens in relation to biting incidents and share up-to-date, accurate information with teachers and parents.

- Work closely to support the teachers to be skilled, knowledgeable professionals by providing additional information, such as new strategies to respond to biting, and resources, such as an extra staff member at transition times, and reminding them of other difficult program situations that have been overcome by everyone working together.

- Conduct event sampling, time sampling, and a review of incident reports to document the antecedents to biting, the most effective consequences, and the frequency of biting at different times of day, and then develop targeted strategies to respond.

- With written parental permission, conduct developmental screening when biting and other behaviors are extreme and indicate a need for additional assessment and professional intervention.

- Link parents to community resources to reduce family stress that might exhibit itself in biting or other acting-out behaviors in the child.

- Assist parents with referrals to alternate care when needed.

Responses to avoid:

- Dismiss a child based solely on considerations of the impact on program tuition.

- Abandon a child and family who have been working in partnership with the program.

- Ignore the concerns of teachers and/or parents about children's behavior or the level of supervision in the program.

- Confirm or deny the name of a biter or any child involved in an incident report, even when asked directly by a parent, as this would be a breach of confidentiality.

- Fail to prepare parents for this challenging stage of toddler development or to follow up with "when most needed" help and information.

- Imagine your program to be the only program that could provide the care needed by a particular child.

For more information on effective responses to children who exhibit biting and other harmful or difficult behaviors, go to these Web sites:

http://www.vh.org

http://www.beckybailey.com/

http://www.wevas.ca/

ISSUES AND TRENDS

CHILD ABUSE AND NEGLECT

According to the National Clearinghouse on Child Abuse and Neglect Information, more than 900,000 children were determined to be victims of abuse or neglect in 2003. Although the rate of victimization in the national population has shown a slight improvement, dropping from 13.4 children per 1,000 in 1990 to 12.4 children per 1,000 in 2003, child abuse and neglect continues to be a major concern with an estimated 1,500 children killed as a result of maltreatment in 2003. Early childhood educators and child care providers are often on the frontline of recognizing and responding to child abuse and neglect. Administrators need to understand this problem and the role of early childhood programs in preventing and reducing child abuse and neglect. Administrators must be certain that new staff members receive training and orientation to help them identify and report child abuse and neglect. This training must also make staff members aware of their legal obligations as mandated reporters and help them recognize how to support a stressed parent who may be at risk of abusing or neglecting his or her child. It must also convince staff members of the vital role that they can play in protecting children from maltreatment.

What you can do:

- Familiarize yourself with terms used in discussing child abuse and neglect and with the causes and indicators of abuse and neglect.

- Document and report suspected child abuse and neglect in accordance with state and federal requirements.

- Provide all staff members with printed information at hire on identifying, reporting, and preventing child abuse and neglect, including their legal responsibilities as care and education providers.

- Require a signed commitment from staff members at hire to follow through on legal obligations to report and keep a copy in each employee's personnel file.

- Provide all staff members with more detailed training regarding child abuse and neglect within their probationary period and update this training during annual in-service training as needed, based on changes in law and knowledge of best practices.

- Create a written policy and procedure for your program outlining detailed steps for responding to suspected child abuse and neglect, including procedures for responding to allegations against program personnel.

- Educate your local community about child abuse and neglect and advocate for programs that serve to help families and reduce the risk of abuse, neglect, or even abandonment.

QUALITY AND AFFORDABILITY

Child care teachers and administrators are faced with the challenge of providing high-quality care and education while operating within realistic budgets and keeping child care affordable for working families. Whether a child care program is publicly funded, a private not-for-profit program, part of a national corporate chain, or a small, local for-profit child care center, teachers and administrators alike must make the most of their resources. Child care personnel must often work with a level of professional dedication that exceeds what is usually expected for their wage or salary range to continue to raise quality while maintaining affordability.

What you can do:

- Understand that financing is fundamental to every other issue in early childhood care and education programs.

- Learn to understand, create, and manage budgets and to use a budget spreadsheet program.

- Calculate the true cost of quality for your child care program, that is, what it would cost to provide care that is consistent with NAEYC accreditation standards.

- Educate staff and parents on current budget realities, the true cost of quality, and the relationship between financing and program improvement.

- Set funding the true cost of quality as a long-term goal for your program and set short-term incremental goals to manage expenses and increase revenues to work toward this long-term goal.

- Involve center personnel at every level in making the most of existing resources, eliminating waste, and finding creative money-savers that do not reduce quality.

- Create a climate of shared decision-making in which every teacher, assistant teacher, and support person is considered a leader and has a voice in influencing significant financial decisions.

- Make annual incremental adjustments to tuition and fees rather than large adjustments spaced several years apart.

- Network with local businesses and involve business partners in sponsoring and supporting your program.

- Learn about fund-raising, donor development, and grant writing and use these methods to increase revenue streams for your program.

- Explore subsidies, scholarships, and other strategies to make space in high-quality programs available to children regardless of family income.

- Develop multiple revenue streams for your child care program and avoid relying on a single revenue stream such as government funded subsidies.

- Learn about worthy wage campaigns and other projects to close the gap between quality and affordability nationwide and join with families and other early childhood educators to advocate for systemic change in child care funding.

For more information, visit the NAEYC Web site at http://www.naeyc.org.

LITERACY

From their earliest relationships at home and in their child care programs, children are building the knowledge, skills, and attitudes needed for literacy, equipping them to make the most of school and to become lifelong learners. The No Child Left Behind Act of 2001 focused national attention on improving children's scores in reading and in math, which is heavily dependent on reading ability. States such as Florida have followed this emphasis by requiring all child care personnel to complete basic coursework in fostering early literacy. At the same time, many educators are concerned that too much emphasis on drilling isolated literacy skills combined with a culture that is increasingly focused on computer-based communication will create a nation of children who are able to read, but rarely choose to open a book. Teachers and administrators can work together with families to build each young child's vocabulary; to provide rich, playful, interesting learning experiences related to literature; to develop an awareness and understanding of print; to awaken ability with the sounds of letters and words; to nurture enjoyment of reading and writing; and to show children how books take them "beyond the screen."

What you can do:

- Include an on-the-spot written response item in all teaching staff interviews to hire staff members who can express themselves in writing.

- Include an item related to knowledge of developmentally appropriate children's literature in all teaching staff interviews.

- Ask every applicant for a teaching position (including assistant teachers) to read aloud a children's picture book as if they were reading it to a group of two-year-olds as part of their interview.

- Demonstrate lap and small group reading for all classroom volunteers as part of their volunteer orientation process.

- Model all aspects of literacy to staff, families, and children in your program; talk about a great article you read at a parent meeting; chat about a great beach read at lunch with staff; write clear, easy-to-understand informative memos and newsletter items; sit in with children and read your book at quiet reading times; and write encouraging notes to school-agers in your program.

- Ensure that teachers receive training and professional development in supporting early literacy for young children.

- Provide workshops, one-sheet handouts, and newsletter items for families that inform them on how they can support their children's early literacy.

- Select curricula that use developmentally appropriate practice to develop early literacy knowledge and skills including hands-on, purposeful classroom and take-home activities and center-family events that involve families in nurturing "readers and writers."

- Provide teachers with the materials they need to create a print-rich environment throughout the program, to teach phonological awareness, and to build alphabetic knowledge.

- Provide a literature-rich environment with appropriate books and magazines in all learning centers.

- Connect books and creative writing activities to children's interests, including their television, movie, and computer interests.

- Make opportunities for listening, talking, reading, and writing part of all day and everyday experiences for the children.

CHILDHOOD OBESITY

Over the past 30 years, the incidence of obesity has dramatically increased among children in the United States. Results from the 1999–2002 National Health and Nutrition Examination Survey indicate that an estimated 16% of children and adolescents 6–19 are overweight. Children with this level of obesity are at far greater risk of continuing to be obese in adulthood; have an alarming increase in Type 2 diabetes; have high cholesterol and blood pressure levels, putting them at risk for heart disease; and suffer other serious health risks such as sleep apnea and asthma. Early childhood programs can work in partnership with families to prevent obesity by promoting healthy eating, activity, and rest patterns.

After unhealthy patterns are established in early childhood and the elementary years, it is notoriously difficult to change those behaviors. Early childhood programs play a vital role in providing a healthy start for children and alleviating the epidemic of obesity currently affecting children in our society.

What you can do:

- Provide healthy, well-balanced meal plans for children in your care focusing on recommended servings of fruits, vegetables, and calcium-rich foods.

- Do not serve foods high in fats, salt, or sugar.

- Do not serve soda and do limit servings of fruit juices.

- Be sure that children have enough water to drink throughout the day.

- Provide family-style meals with adults eating healthy foods alongside children and warm, nurturing conversation as part of the mealtime.

- Teach children how to prepare and serve their own healthy foods.

- Provide many interesting opportunities for movement and activity throughout the day both indoors and outdoors.

- Foster noncompetitive games and sports for elementary-age children where everyone can participate and no one is "benched."

- Arrange more walkable field trips and fewer trips that require driving.

- Limit "screen time" to truly educational opportunities for preschoolers and young school-agers (television, DVDs, videos, computers, electronic games) and avoid "screen time" altogether for children under the age of three.

- Never use television and videos as a "babysitter."

- Provide rest time; evidence is accumulating that links sleep deprivation with weight gain.

- Educate staff members and families on healthy nutrition, activity, and rest as well as the dangers of childhood obesity.

- Be a great role model of healthy eating, exercising, and resting.

- Advocate for safe, attractive, well-supervised outdoor areas for children to play in the community.

- Do not use or withhold physical activity as a form of punishment.

- Provide opportunities for children and family members to be active together as part of your program.

For more information, search these Web sites:

http://www.nih.gov

http://obesity.org

http://mypyramid.gov

http://www.ers.usda.gov

ASSESSMENT AND EVALUATION

Child care teachers and administrators need to be aware of whether or not the program they are providing is effective for each of the children in their care. What is working well in the program and what needs to be changed? How can good programs be made even better? It is important for teachers and administrators to understand measures for the screening and assessment of individual children. Teachers and administrators also need to be comfortable using tools that examine the effectiveness and quality of the program as a whole to enhance the care and education provided. Teachers and administrators need to develop their competence in using developmental checklists, writing anecdotal and running records, and conducting time and event samples. Children also benefit when programs make effective use of portfolio assessment, compiling a detailed picture of each child's growth and progress over time. At least some staff members should be skilled in administering developmental screening instruments such as the ASQ (Ages and Stages Questionnaire), the ESI-R (Early Screening Inventory-Revised), or the LAP-D (Learning Accomplishment Profile-Diagnostic).

Administrators and key staff members also need to be knowledgeable about the characteristics of high-quality screening instruments. A good screening instrument is "user friendly" for children and teachers, has excellent statistical validity and reliability, is suitable for the particular population to be screened, is affordable, helps to build rather than damage a partnership with parents, and has individual screening items, which minimize cultural bias.

Administrators and teachers also need to be familiar with procedures for referring children for further assessment by professionals beyond the early childhood education program when screening results indicate that this could benefit the child. Assessment of individual children's progress combined with evaluation of overall program quality can give teachers and administrators the facts they require to advocate for resources that will help to meet all children's needs.

What you can do:

- Attend training on screening, assessment, and evaluation tools both for measuring the progress of individual children and for measuring the quality and effectiveness of the program.

- Ensure that teachers receive training on the screening, assessment, and evaluation tools they will use, including confidentiality requirements for handling information about individual children and families.

- Educate families in the program about developmentally appropriate screening, assessment, and evaluation purposes and methods.

- Conduct needs assessment to discern which tools and methods are best suited to your program's needs.

- Select tools that fit the needs of the children and families in your care, match your curriculum, and provide for enhancement of individual and program-wide educational plans.

- Implement a coordinated, systematic approach to screening, assessment, and evaluation in your program with well-documented, confidential records and timely monitoring of individual children's progress as well as overall program quality.

- Coordinate and cooperate with local agencies and institutions such as local colleges, child care resource and referral agencies, and public school systems, which can offer resources, technical assistance, and interventions to enhance the program and support the development of individual children.

■ Link feedback from use of program assessment tools such as NAEYC accreditation or the ECERS (Early Childhood Environmental Rating Scale) to curriculum planning and budget projection.

■ Incorporate child and program assessment data into grant applications and advocacy discussions to enhance programs for children.

For more information, search these Web sites:

http://www.naeyc.org

http://www.fpg.unc.edu

http://www.brookespublishing.com

http://www.kaplanco.com

TECHNOLOGY

A generation ago, early childhood educators were wary of computers and other technological innovations that seemed alien to the early childhood classroom. Now computers, cell phones, digital cameras, scanners, and other technological innovations are a reality in the early childhood classroom and are essential components of the day-to-day operation of a child care center. Teachers and administrators need to be prepared to stay up to date with technological developments to prepare the children in their care for the increasingly high-tech future in which they will be adults. They need to know how to use computers, digital cameras, and assistive technologies as creative resources for cooperative learning and developmentally appropriate practice for 21st-century children. They also need to know how to use technology for their own professional development, program management, and communication with families and the community.

What you can do:

■ Become competent in using up-to-date word processing, spreadsheet, presentation, program management, publishing, and communications computer applications.

- Provide opportunities and incentives for all staff to become computer literate and competent.

- Facilitate online training opportunities for staff.

- Make the program a hub for the development of computer literacy and competence for families enrolled in the program by providing on-site workshops, computer lab, and so on.

- Incorporate computers and developmentally appropriate software into early childhood classrooms to promote both independent and cooperative learning.

- Stay up to date on hardware and software innovations, on computer-based resources, and on current and proposed uses of technology in the early childhood field.

- Seek opportunities for technology to overcome barriers and solve problems; for example, create a chat room for program families and have "online parent nights" to overcome the challenges of bringing everyone in for a meeting.

- Put technology in the hands of children for exciting hands-on learning experiences; for example, use digital cameras with young school-agers to promote creative writing and reflective thinking.

- Become familiar with assistive technology devices that will benefit children with special needs in your program.

- Be selective in your use of new technology focusing on innovations that fit your program's needs and support developmentally appropriate practice; for example, consider whether or not your program really needs a Web site.

- Monitor and preview all materials (videos, DVDs, audio tapes, computer software, etc.) that will be used for and by children in the program to ensure that they do not promote violence and aggression or contain other inappropriate content.

- Balance time spent with technology with time spent using messy creative materials, exploring outdoors, and enjoying many other aspects of childhood.

- Avoid screen technology (television, DVDs/videos, and computers) for children under the age of two.

For more information, search this Web site:

http://www.aap.org

CULTURAL AND LINGUISTIC DIVERSITY

Cultural and linguistic diversity is a reality in many child care programs. Even in the most homogeneous communities, teachers and administrators eventually find themselves working with a family from a culture different from their own, a family whose members speak a language with which the staff members are unfamiliar. Teachers and administrators in large, urban settings may be working with colleagues, families, and children from multiple cultures who speak many different languages. Cultural and linguistic diversity can add complexity to issues that are already challenging; for example, different cultures may have contrasting approaches to child discipline or to gender roles, while language barriers may add confusion to efforts to communicate. Teachers and administrators who develop an understanding and appreciation of cultural and linguistic diversity, who learn how to support a wide variety of children and families, and who are able to teach children to understand and appreciate each other can help all children to succeed and enrich their community.

What you can do:

- Through workshops, travel, and interpersonal experiences, learn about a wide variety of cultures; get to know one culture other than your birth culture in depth.

- Become familiar with the anti-bias curriculum approach.

- Provide opportunities and incentives for staff to learn about a variety of cultures and explore antibias curriculum.

- Provide materials, furnishings, and equipment that reflect and extend the cultures present in your program.

- Provide events and communications that celebrate the cultures present in the program.

- Seek contributions and resources from representatives of all the cultures in the program. Ask "who else needs to be at the table?" when making changes and decisions.

- Recruit and hire staff members from a variety of cultures who are bilingual and multilingual, which will help you to recruit and enroll children from a variety of cultures who speak a variety of languages.

- Remember that cultures are not only bounded by nationality or ethnicity, but also by other features such as physical abilities and regional identity. Be sensitive to these cultural differences, too.

- Consider cultural variance when working with challenges such as child abuse, while always giving first priority to legal and ethical commitments to the child.

- Make education about the history and wealth of each culture a year-round, all-day, every-day part of your program, not limited to a specific month or day.

- Introduce elements of ESOL (English for Speakers of Other Languages) teacher training in your program.

- Demonstrate respect for people of all cultures and seek commonalities while acknowledging differences.

For more information, search this Web site for topics related to antibias curriculum:

http://www.answers.com